Sprout

*21 Days for the Fruit of the Spirit
to Bloom in Your Life*

Sprout: *21 Days for the Fruit of the Spirit to Bloom in Your Life*

Copyright © 2023 by Gateway Publishing®

Written by Robert Morris, Jelani Lewis, Josh Morris, Claire Jennings, Dana Stone, Zac Rowe, Hannah Etsebeth, Bridgette Morris, Sion Alford, Monica Bates, Thomas Miller, Kyle Fox, James Morris, Casey Hale, Elizabeth Settle, Tom Lane, Dr. Irini Fambro, Todd Lane, Chelsea Seaton, Elisabeth Dunn, and Matthew Hernandez.

Editorial Director *S. George Thomas*

Executive Director Gateway Media *Lawrence Swicegood*

Senior Director Gateway Publishing *Stacy Burnett*

Senior Editors *Jenny Morgan, Katie Smith*

Project Coordinator *Chasity Walker*

Creative Director *Peyton Sepeda*

Designer *Emanuel Puşcaş*

ISBN: 978-1-956943-52-8

We hope you hear from the Holy Spirit and receive God's richest blessings from this devotional by Gateway Publishing. Our purpose is to carry out the mission and vision of Gateway Church through print and digital resources to equip leaders, disciple believers, and advance God's kingdom. For more information on other resources from Gateway Publishing® go to GatewayPublishing.com.

GatewayPublishing.com | GatewayDevotions.com | GatewayPeople.com

Printed in the United States of America | Miklis Printing, Inc., Garland, Texas (miklis.com)

Contents

Love *is the Christlike reaction to people's malice.*

Joy *is the Christlike reaction to depressing circumstances.*

Peace *is the Christlike reaction to troubles, threats, and invitations to anxiety.*

Patience *is the Christlike reaction to all that is maddening.*

Kindness *is the Christlike reaction to all that are unkind.*

Goodness *is the Christlike reaction to bad people and bad behavior.*

Faithfulness and gentleness *are the Christlike reactions to lies and fury.*

Self-control *is the Christlike reaction to every situation that goads you to lose your cool and hit out.*

J.I. PACKER

1

Abide in Me

By Robert Morris

Abide in Me, and I in you. As the branch cannot bear fruit of itself, unless it abides in the vine, neither can you, unless you abide in Me. I am the vine, you are the branches. He who abides in Me, and I in him, bears much fruit; for without Me you can do nothing.

JOHN 15:4-5

When I was growing up, my dad owned an engineering company that performed land surveying. At just eight years old, I started surveying with him on weekends. He'd give me a machete (not sure I'd give any of my kids or grandkids a machete at that age!) and teach me how to cut vines and branches that were in the way of the property line. I remember early on my dad told me to watch out for the "wait a minute" vine. Obviously, that's not the official name of the vine; it's just what we called them because you'd be walking along and then get caught in the vine's thorns and have to yell, "Wait a minute!"

In the Gospel of John, Jesus says, "I am the vine, you are the branches. He who abides in Me, and I in him, bears much fruit; for without Me you can do nothing" (John 15:5). He doesn't mean He's a prickly "wait a minute" vine. He also doesn't mean He's the kind of vine you'd find Tarzan swinging on in the jungle. The word vine in this verse is translated as "grapevine." So Jesus is really saying that He's a fruit-producing grapevine. And what kind of fruit does He produce? "Love, joy, peace, patience, kindness, goodness, faithfulness, gentleness, and self-control"—the fruit of His Spirit (Galatians 5:22–23 NLT).

It's interesting to note that when a grapevine goes through a struggle or experiences adversity, such as extreme weather conditions, the vine produces heartier and healthier grapes, which in turn result in a higher quality of wine. The same is true of people. People who bear really good fruit are the ones who remain in a committed relationship with Christ when they're pressed or go through a struggle. They display kindness when they could easily complain. They stay faithful and loving when their marriage goes through a difficult season. They show self-control when they're mistreated. They demonstrate patience when their children have to learn the same lessons over and over. They stay connected to the Vine—Jesus—and it shows through the sweetness of their fruit.

So what does Jesus mean when He says those who abide in Him *bear* much fruit? You might think this word means "to produce," yet it actually means "to carry." There's quite a difference between these two! As the Vine, Jesus is the only one who can *produce* the fruit. That's not our responsibility—we just *carry* it. Think about a fruit tree. If you cut off a single branch, it stops producing fruit, and eventually, it dies. But when that branch *remains* connected to the rest of the tree, it eventually *bears* fruit.

Similarly, those who stay connected to Jesus—to the Vine—bear fruit, while those who don't abide in Him "can do nothing." That's pretty clear language, right? Yet we so often think that if we just try hard enough and use all our might, we can somehow produce fruit on a broken branch! No, Jesus says the key to bearing the fruit of His Spirit is the word *abide*. But what does this really mean? The word *abide* means to "stay in one place for a long time." And the root of the word implies staying through struggle or adversity.

So *why* is it important to stay connected to the Vine when we face challenges in life? It doesn't matter whether the challenge is relational, financial, mental, or physical—whatever it is, it's *vital* to stay connected to Jesus because He *alone* is the source of all life. When we *aren't* connected to Him, we wither up and die.

However, when we *do* abide in Jesus, pressing in and staying connected to Him when things are good *and* when things are bad, we bear sweet, appealing fruit. This serves two incredible purposes. The first is to display God's nature to the world. And the second is so people can eat it! In other words, simply by encountering you or being in relationship with you, people can "taste and see that the Lord is good!" (See Psalm 34:8.) They can see the fruit of the Spirit in your life.

Throughout the remaining 20 days of this devotional, you'll read encouraging stories and principles from various writers about how the Holy Spirit produces the fruit of love, joy, peace, patience, kindness, goodness, faithfulness, gentleness, and self-control in your life. You'll discover areas of your life where you're already displaying this fruit and areas where you can grow and mature. You'll learn there's more to the fruit of the Spirit than just being nice. But if you only remember *one* thing from this 21-day journey, remember this: **abide in the Vine**. You don't need to *produce* the fruit of the Spirit in your life; you simply need to *bear* it. And if you abide in Him—if you stay constantly connected to Jesus through struggle and hardship as well as prosperity and abundance—the more fruit you'll carry to a dark and broken world.

PRAYER

Jesus, I confess that You are the Vine, and I am just a branch. I cannot produce any of the fruit of Your Spirit on my own, but when I am connected to You, I can bear love, joy, peace, patience, kindness, goodness, faithfulness, gentleness, and self-control. Help me to abide in You always—even through tough times. And let other people see this fruit and come to know You. In Jesus' name, Amen.

FOR FURTHER STUDY

Matthew 7:16–18; 2 Corinthians 5:17; James 1:2–4; John 14:6

FOR FURTHER REFLECTION

1. Have you ever tried to produce the fruit of the Spirit in your own strength? How did that go? What could you do differently next time?

2. Think about a time you stayed close to God during adversity. What fruit came out of that season? Did people notice? What did you learn?

HOLY SPIRIT,
WHAT ARE YOU
SAYING TO
ME TODAY?

2

The Love Card

By Jelani Lewis

Dear friends, let us continue to love one another, for love comes from God. Anyone who loves is a child of God and knows God. But anyone who does not love does not know God, for God is love.

1 JOHN 4:7-8 NLT

My wife and I have been married for just over a decade. We met when I interviewed her to be my assistant. (Don't judge me! The Lord works in mysterious ways.) She and I laugh about it now because she technically turned me down for the job, but thankfully, she accepted me for life! Anyway, a few months after our wedding, an older pastor provided a profound piece of marital advice. She said, "When you get married, it's like God hands you two playing cards. One card is the 'love' card, and the other one is the 'change' card. If you choose to play the change card on your spouse (meaning you spend your time, effort, and energy trying to change them or make them into what you think they should be), it's like God says, 'Well fine, then I'll just love them.' However, if you choose to play the love card (meaning you spend your time, effort, and energy on how to best love your spouse), then God says, 'Great. Now I'll have the opportunity to change you both.'"

What's interesting is there isn't a single instance in Scripture when God calls us to change anyone. Yes, we are called to be influential light in a dark world. Yes, we are exhorted to be a city on a hill. And yes, our commission is to make disciples. However, what we won't find are Scriptures that say, "Beloved, let us change one another," or "A new command I give to you: as I have modified you, you should modify one another." Or my personal favorite: "Fix thy neighbor." I may have missed it on the YouVersion Bible app somewhere, but making people into what *we* want or think they *should* be isn't found anywhere in the Holy Scriptures.

However, what we *do* find is a clear command to love. The apostle John writes in 1 John 4:7–8, "Dear friends, let us continue to love one another, for love comes from God. Anyone who loves is a child of God and knows God. But anyone who does not love does not know God, for God is love." Paul also echoes this sentiment when he encourages the believers at Corinth on the importance of love and helps them understand exactly what loving people looks like: "Love is patient and kind. Love is not jealous or boastful or proud or rude. It does not demand its own way. It is not irritable, and it keeps no record of being wronged. It does not rejoice about injustice but rejoices whenever the truth wins out. Love never gives up, never loses faith, is always hopeful, and endures through every circumstance" (1 Corinthians 13:4–7 NLT).

Jesus even challenges His disciples in Luke 6:35 to "love your enemies!" This doesn't mean we resign ourselves to simply being a door mat. Nor does it mean we never address an issue or set a boundary. On the contrary, sometimes the most loving thing we can do is set a boundary or speak the truth in love. Nevertheless, regardless of the situation, the question isn't "How can I change them?" The question is "What does love look like?" And the great thing is, love is a fruit of the Spirit, which means if we submit to the leading of the Holy Spirit and stay intimately connected to Jesus, God actually produces His love in us.

Like every couple, my wife and I have had our share of "animated" conversations over the years. Often the moments of my greatest frustration arise because she operates differently than I do (and of course, my way must be the right way). In the aftermath of those discussions, when I pause to listen to the Holy Spirit, He often whispers a simple question: "What does love look like?" The times I have chosen the love card, by the grace of God, I have seen Him do a work in my heart that often leads to transformation in both of us.

So today, let's imagine we have been given two cards. Instead of trying to change everyone, what if we decide to submit to the Spirit, stay connected to Jesus, and simply love. Love our spouse, our children, and our siblings. Love our colleagues, classmates, and neighbors. And yes, even love our enemies. After all, if we play the love card, we might just give God an opportunity to change us all.

PRAYER

Father, thank You for the gift of the Holy Spirit. Today, I submit to the leading of Your Spirit, and as I do, may Your love be produced in me. Help me choose today not to attempt to change everyone, but by Your grace, to love them. In Jesus' name, Amen.

FOR FURTHER STUDY

John 15:9–14; 1 Peter 4:7–9; Luke 6:27–36

1. *Ask the Holy Spirit if He is asking you to love someone whom you have focused on changing.*

2. *What is one practical way you may be able to express love toward that person today?*

> HOLY SPIRIT,
> WHAT ARE YOU
> SAYING TO
> ME TODAY?

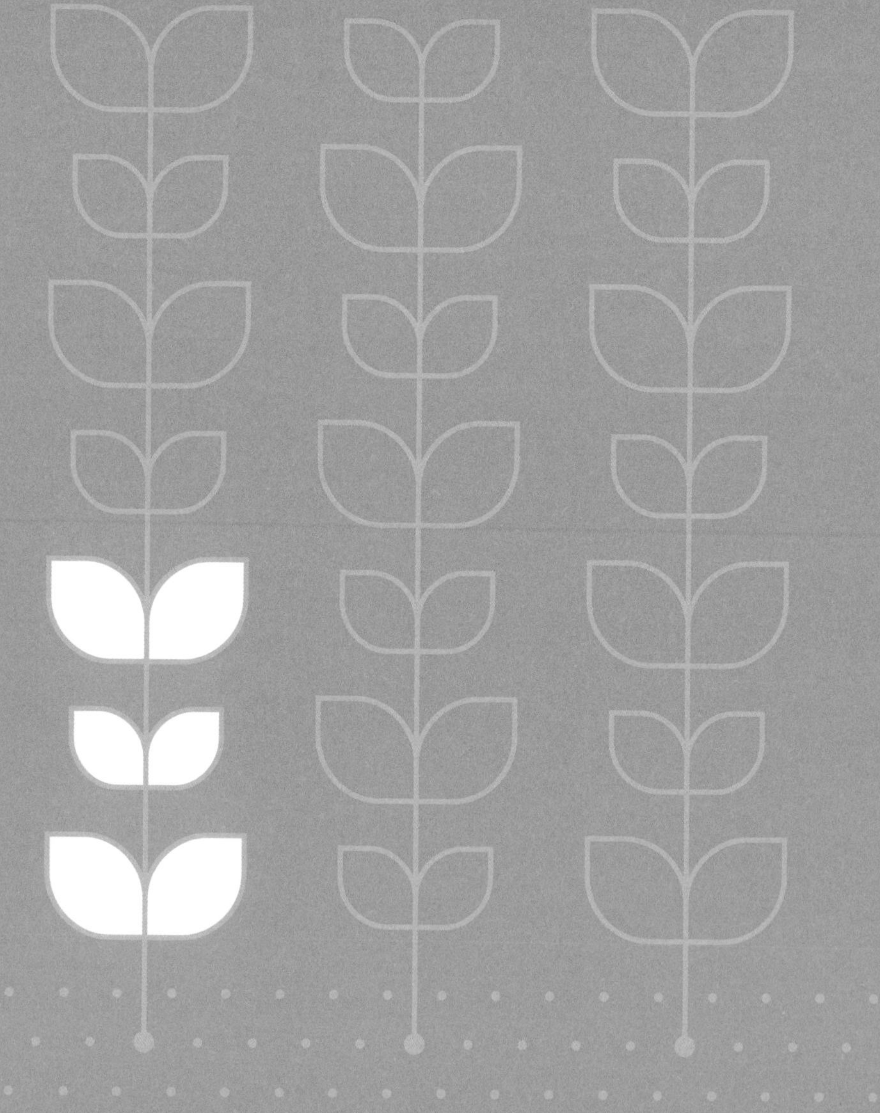

3

Love Is a Calling

By Josh Morris

That they all may be one, as You, Father, are in Me, and I in You; that they also may be one in Us, that the world may believe that You sent Me.

JOHN 17:21

Our phones buzzed at the same time, and my wife, Hannah, and I reluctantly glanced at our screens, assuming it would be something about work or possibly the kids needing something from us. But the very next moment, we realized it wasn't that at all. We had just been invited to visit our friends and stay at their house—*in St. Croix in the Virgin Islands!* We love these friends dearly and would have gone to visit them anywhere, but we were also so excited about getting some beach time.

While we were in St. Croix, Hannah and I integrated ourselves into our friends' family and daily lives. We experienced one of the best and most enjoyable trips we have ever been on, and as I was reflecting on the trip on the flight home, I realized we had witnessed something very special indeed.

For starters, I realized that while I glamorized life on the island, the truth is our friends are very hard workers. Yes, they made good use of the beauty around them, but they also had many hurdles to overcome in establishing a life there and many inconveniences we take for granted here at home. This is a family of extremely hard workers, and the laid-back island life I had imagined was far from the actual reality. They were in a daily battle just like everyone else I know. The same kind of battle we are *all* familiar with—one where you're creating your life and things don't come easy.

The second thing I realized is in the midst of the daily grind, and especially with the isolation that often comes with island life, our friends prioritize family in a way I will never forget. Every individual in their family has a strong personality, and they differ in their thoughts and beliefs and sometimes clash, as is common in every family. However, their priority always remains centered around their family and helping each other out. I watched as they sat at the dinner table and talked about difficult subjects while still having complete certainty that they were family and *nothing* would come between them. They are

a blended family, but you would never guess it by the way they love and care for each other. Their commitment to family is about just that—*commitment*. It is not conditional, and because of that, there is a confidence that they will love each other and have each other's back despite any minor disagreements they may have.

Make no mistake, we live in a harshly divisive time, and the world has come to know conditional love intimately. One minute you are loved, and the next minute you're hated simply because your views vary from someone else's opinions. This toxic worldview reiterates a feeling that love is conditional and if you mess up or disagree with someone, you could lose it all.

There's no question that we as believers are called to love the world and show them what the love of Christ looks like. And that certainly helps to remedy this fragile love that exists all around us. But there is one prayer—and only one—Jesus prayed that we can answer. In John 17:20–23, Jesus prayed that all of us as believers would be one with each other just as He is one with the Father. In fact, He says that when we foster this type of unity among our fellow believers, it stands as the testimony that Jesus is God and was sent by the Father.

This is a heavy calling and one we ought to take much more seriously. The fastest and most effective way of destroying a movement or a group of people is to get them to fight internally so they rot from the inside. Then, by the time you attack them, there is no unity to strengthen them against the onslaught. This is what the Church has done in recent years as we have divided ourselves into more and more subcategories of belief. Now, we often distinguish ourselves not in the ways we are different from the secular world but instead in the ways we are different from each other. Unity is severely lacking in the Church, and because of this, we are not faithfully answering the prayer Jesus prayed for us.

As I watched our friends care for their family and find ways to express their love no matter the temporal disagreement, I realized they were standing as a true testimony to me of what the love of Christ looks like. They are a group of people who loves well and keeps family as a priority over all else.

Maybe we as the Church could learn from their example in this day and age. Maybe we could start seeing believers as fellow family members and servants of the true king. Just maybe, if we can get there, we can start answering the prayer that Jesus prayed over us. This will be the sign to unbelievers and the thing that sets us apart from the world. It's a thing called love, and we are called to be ministers of love so that everyone will know just how strong the love of Christ really is. It overcomes all things. Today, let's choose to love and show the world who God is.

PRAYER

Lord, we ask that You would give us the strength to love our family of believers even when it does not come naturally. Let us resist the worldly temptation to continue to divide, and instead give us the ministry of reconciliation. May we answer Your cry for unity here on earth just as it is in heaven. In Jesus' name, Amen.

FOR FURTHER STUDY

1 Corinthians 13; Colossians 3:14; John 17:22–26; 1 John 4:7–21

1. *What friends, family members, or public figures do you look to as examples of God's love? What specific words or actions draw you to them?*

2. *How can you approach potentially difficult topics with love?*

HOLY SPIRIT,
WHAT ARE YOU
SAYING TO
ME TODAY?

The Choice Is Yours

By Claire Jennings

Always be full of joy in the Lord. I say it again—rejoice!
PHILIPPIANS 4:4 NLT

I remember watching as my 10-year-old niece attempted a penalty kick in her soccer game. There wasn't much time left on the clock, and the game was tied 3–3. She jogged a few steps, kicked the ball, and made it just over the goalie's head. We all screamed and ran around like crazy people! The joy on my niece's face as things went exactly how she wanted them to go is now a memory our family talks about all the time.

Would that moment have looked different had she missed the goal? Absolutely. Sometimes things don't go how we hope for them to, or we miss the goals we are aiming for with all our strength. And if we're honest, joy seems nowhere to be found within those moments.

I once heard a pastor say, "Joy is often the determined choice to praise God." This tells me that while joy is sometimes felt, more often joy is a choice. It goes beyond a fleeting feeling in a positive moment. If you were to change the word joy into a verb, it would be the word "rejoice."

As believers, the Bible instructs us to *choose* to rejoice in the face of difficulty. Our response doesn't simply "happen" to us; no, we have the divinely appointed ability to choose it.

Sometimes joy comes naturally, but other times we have to muster it up from deep within our soul and spirit. Joy stems from knowing who God is rather than who we are or what is going on around us. I remember telling a friend about an uncomfortable new season I was stepping into and not knowing which direction to pursue. She looked at me with a smile and said, "God is good! Aren't transitions fun?" I smiled, and she prayed with me. I walked away from that moment knowing I had desperately needed to hear my friend's words. Through the power of the Holy Spirit inside of her, she found joy in difficult situations, and she was encouraging me to do the same. My friend taught me how to rejoice even when I felt so unsure about the future. She showed me how to look at my situation and choose joy.

I encourage you to dig deep today. Decide that today truly is the day the Lord has made, and you *will* rejoice and be glad in it (see Psalm 118:24). Fill in the blank of whatever circumstance you are facing and depend on God for the courage to rejoice in the face of it. The way to do this is by knowing and trusting who God is.

If you are struggling to find joy today, ask the Holy Spirit these questions and then write down the answers you hear:

- Who is God?

- How much does He love me?

- Has He given me the strength to choose joy today?

Ask the Lord to help you, and be prepared to be amazed as you watch Him fill you with supernatural joy from the crown of your head to the tips of your toes.

PRAYER

Lord, You are my source of joy. I know You care for me better than anyone else ever could. Thank You that I can always count on You. Help me to lean into the Holy Spirit and experience the joy that You so freely offer–even in moments when I don't feel it. I know Your plans for me are good, and today I choose joy over the other feelings I am experiencing. I fix my eyes on You, and I rejoice in your faithfulness today!

In Jesus' name, Amen.

FOR FURTHER STUDY

Psalm 118:24; Psalm 13:5–6;
Psalm 71:23

FOR FURTHER REFLECTION

1. *Find four Scriptures you can reference when you need joy and put them in an accessible place (lock screen on your phone, notecard on your bathroom mirror, etc.). The more you read and recite theses verses, the more the truth of God's Word will bring joy into your heart even when you don't feel it.*

2. *Ask the Lord to help you find joy in the moments you need it each day. Declare joy over yourself, and watch the difference it makes in every area of your life.*

HOLY SPIRIT,
WHAT ARE YOU
SAYING TO
ME TODAY?

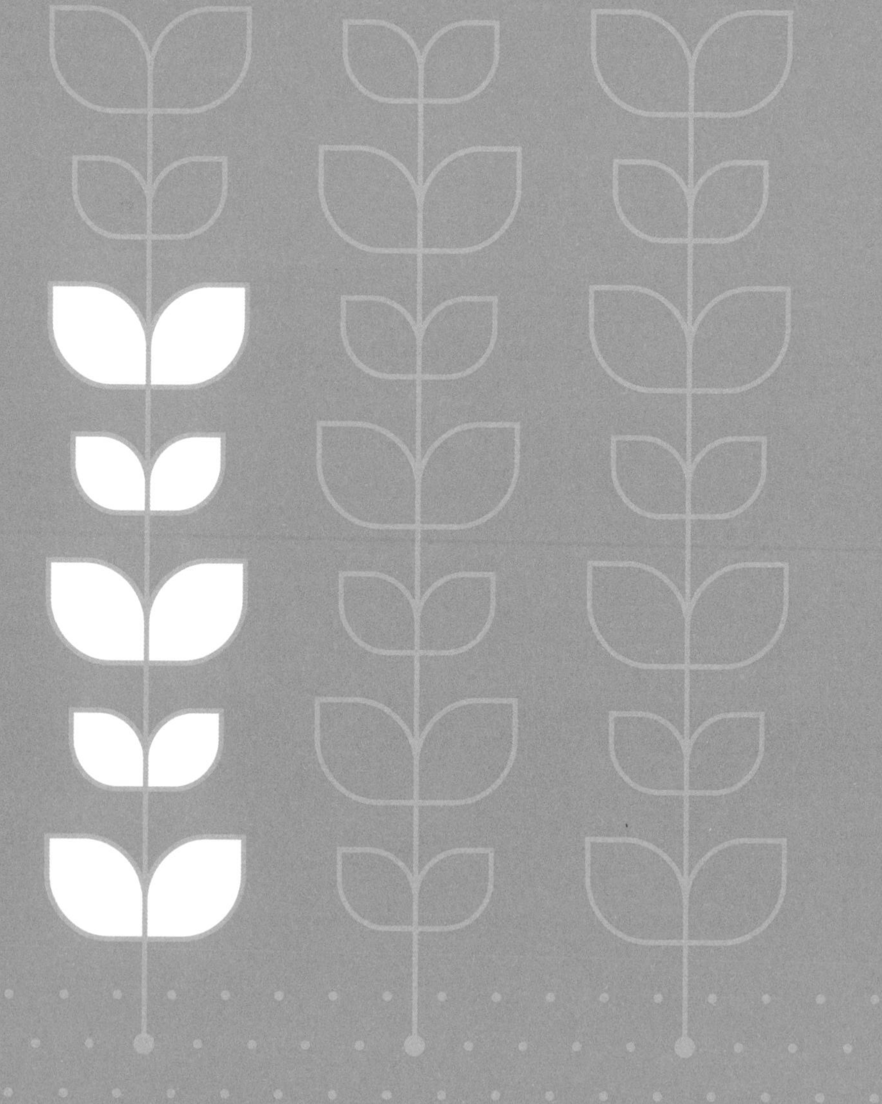

5

A Sweet Fragrance

By Dana Stone

*And now just as you trusted Christ to save you, trust him, too,
for each day's problems; live in vital union with him. Let your
roots grow down into him and draw up nourishment from him.
See that you go on growing in the Lord, and become strong and
vigorous in the truth you were taught. Let your lives overflow
with joy and thanksgiving for all he has done.*

COLOSSIANS 2:6-7 TLB

I answered the phone at 7:30 that morning, knowing what my brother was about to say. It was time. I hurriedly packed a bag and began the five-hour car ride to join my brother and sister to be with Mom as she made the journey to her eternal home. We spent the next several hours telling her how thankful we were for the gift she had been to us. We shared memories of the incredibly strong yet compassionate woman and mother she had always been. We held her hand as she passed away peacefully that evening, tears of grief and gratitude intermingling as we said our goodbyes. As I drove back to the hotel that night, all I could think to say to the Lord was, "Really God? That's three hands now. What am I supposed to do with all this pain?"

Three hands. In the last eight years, I had held three hands as they made their way home to heaven—my dad, my uncle, and now my mom. Grief overwhelmed me, and I wasn't sure I would be strong enough to make my way through it this time. I wondered if my heart would ever have room for joy again.

As we began to go through Mom's things over the next few days, we found her trusted Bible, and inside was a card marking a page that had Colossians 2:6–7 underlined: "And now just as you trusted Christ to save you, trust him, too, for each day's problems; live in vital union with him. Let your roots grow down into him and draw up nourishment from him. See that you go on growing in the Lord, and become strong and vigorous in the truth you were taught. Let your lives overflow with joy and thanksgiving for all he has done" (TLB). As I soaked in the words written by the apostle Paul, it was as if my mom had left me a final gift—a reminder that no matter what

trials may come in this life, we, as God's children, are rooted in Christ and have been given the gift of the Holy Spirit. As we deepen those roots, the fruit of the Spirit naturally flows out of us. While reading those verses from Colossians, the grief encompassing my heart gradually began to give way to the sweetest presence of joy.

Joy is the quiet, inextinguishable confidence that no matter what we're walking through, God is with us. Whether we're having a mountaintop experience or walking through the lowest valleys of life, His Holy Spirit lifts our hearts and our heads as we learn to abide in His presence and soak in His Word. And as we do, joy has no choice but to burst forth out of the depths of our spirit like a well of refreshing water flowing up from the deepest crevices in the earth. It is that joy—that pure, life-giving water—that allows us to steady our gaze, plant our feet on God's firm foundation, and "go out with joy, and be led forth with peace" (Isaiah 55:12 KJV). Joy will flow out of the wounded places in your heart and enable you to withstand the most difficult circumstances because you can rest in the truth that God is with you every step of the way.

Sitting in Mom's room that day, I made a decision—I would choose to fix my heart on the Lord and remind myself that I wasn't in this alone. Grief would need to run its course, but I knew God was right there with me, and joy would be there too.

Life can be overwhelming at times, and there are natural, normal emotions we will all face. None of us are exempt. But when we choose to allow God to guide us through those difficult seasons by abiding *in* His Word and drawing strength *from* Him, His joy will be the sweet fragrance that remains.

PRAYER

Father, thank You for the gift of Your Holy Spirit. Help me deepen my understanding of Your Word so that the roots of my faith can be strengthened. I ask for the fruit of joy to be evident in my life, in the good times and in the difficult times. May Your joy flow through me, leaving the sweet aroma of Jesus wherever I go. In Jesus' name, Amen.

FOR FURTHER STUDY

Psalm 16:7–9, 11; Psalm 71:23; Acts 2:28; Romans 15:13

1. *Write down three prayers the Lord has answered. Thank Him for His provision and meditate on the joy you experienced in those moments.*

2. *Take a few minutes to be still before the Lord as you read Colossians 2:6–7. Write down a current trial you are experiencing and ask the Holy Spirit for a fresh infilling of His joy. Pray for His power to be released in you so that you can remain in a posture of joy as you navigate that trial.*

HOLY SPIRIT,
WHAT ARE YOU
SAYING TO
ME TODAY?

6

An Invitation

By Zac Rowe

*You keep him in perfect peace whose mind is stayed on you,
because he trusts in you.*

ISAIAH 26:3 ESV

Wind whips through Peter's salty, sea-soaked hair as he squints out into the dark, stormy night. Clinging to the edge of the boat for balance as another murky wave comes crashing over the side, he ignores the whispers of "Ghost!" from his friends in the ship with him and calls out to the figure standing on the waves: "Lord, if it is you, command me to come to you on the water" (Matthew 14:28 ESV). As Peter strains to hear a response over the boat's creaking protests, the raging wind carries back an invitation: "Come" (v. 29).

Imagine that moment of decision—the exact moment when Peter chooses to let go of what he knew about reality and step into a new one. Years of experience as a fisherman had solidified in his mind the scientific truth that man cannot walk on water, and yet here was evidence to the contrary. In this moment, I imagine Peter closing his eyes to the rain and wind. As he considers all the things he's seen the Master do, a strange sense of peace comes over his mind. Firm and immovable as an anchor, this peace holds strong as Peter opens his eyes and steps over the side of the boat into the unknown.

It's important for us to remember that Peter wasn't aware at the time that every child in Sunday school would be taught this story while eating cheesy Goldfish crackers for millennia to come. He didn't know he was living "Matthew 14:22–33" or have the benefit of the caption "Jesus Walks on the Water" glowing in neon lights over the black surging sea. All he knew as the waves beat against the ship was that they were trying their best to drag him into the depths below. Peter had to make his decision not based on evidence in the natural but on an invitation by the Spirit.

We know the story. Peter steps out onto the water and, defying the understood laws of the natural world, walks on the surface of the waves toward Jesus. For those brief, miraculous moments, faith was the only substance beneath his feet.

Today, you and I face our own dark nights—times when following the Lord in obedience leads us into a storm. It's easy to misinterpret dark, stormy seasons of our lives as punishment or rebuke, but just before Peter walked on the water, the Bible says Jesus "made the disciples get into the boat and go before him to the other side" (v. 22). Maybe the storms we walk through are less about limitation and more an invitation—an open door into a new, greater reality with Jesus. As we consider this invitation, it should be noted it is accompanied by a peace that is only known "beyond understanding." The end of our ability to comprehend is not the end of God's ability to carry on in power. When we find ourselves facing situations we've never walked through and trials like oceans in our way, peace is both the guide and the guard for our hearts and minds.

Merriam-Webster defines peace as "freedom from disquieting or oppressive thoughts or emotions." According to Philippians 4:7, God's peace acts like a shield. It stands in the way of the attacks of the enemy when he tries to assault our minds with anxiety and worry for the future. Against all the natural evidence we might muster up as we look at the storm in front of us, peace comes like a heavenly shield through the clarity and calmness of trust.

You see, peace is intimately interwoven with trust. How can we face a difficult time in our lives like the uncertainty and pain of losing a loved one or the difficulty of changing seasons and still have any sense of peace at all? Peace comes because we trust in God's power, presence, and proficiency in working it all out for good. He's currently working on whatever is burdening you, and He doesn't need any help finishing the job.

Just as Peter stood on the precipice of one reality, hearing an invitation into another, you and I stand today at the edge of whatever issue is facing us with the invitation to trust God and take Him at His word. As we trust Him, we'll experience that miraculous feeling of walking on the waves of faith and trust as we journey on toward the prize of Jesus.

---

1 *Merriam-Webster.com Dictionary*, s.v. "peace," accessed September 1, 2022, https://www.merriam-webster.com/dictionary/peace.

PRAYER

God, we honor Your great power over all things. We have witnessed Your authority to speak to the wind and waves of our lives and have seen them obey Your command to be still. Today, until You speak those words and bring whatever is facing us to stillness, teach us to trust You and Your process. You are worthy to be praised and worthy to be trusted. We put all our hope in You alone. In Jesus' Name, Amen.

FOR FURTHER STUDY

Philippians 4:6–7; John 14:27; John 16:33

Imagine a hand that's been balled into a fist. As an act of your will, now picture that hand opening up as you release every tie to worry, anxiety, fear, unbelief, and the stress that you've been gripping so tightly. See the cords of those negative things falling like strings through your fingertips, as you raise your eyes and hands to reach again towards Jesus.

HOLY SPIRIT,
WHAT ARE YOU
SAYING TO
ME TODAY?

7

Exchanged for Peace

By Hannah Etsebeth

Peace I leave with you; my peace I give to you. Not as the world gives do I give to you. Let not your hearts be troubled, neither let them be afraid.

JOHN 14:27 ESV

It was 2010, and my longtime friend-turned-new boyfriend was off to the doctor. He had been having an irregular heartbeat for a few weeks, so he booked an appointment and strapped on a heart monitor. A few days later he sat in front of his doctor to hear the results: "You are completely fine. I suspect you are in love." Six months later we were married, and to this day I remain amused.

Fast forward to 2018, and this time it was *my* heart that was racing, though once again because of love. Well, to be honest, love *and* concern. Our family had just completed a two-and-a-half-year process of adopting our daughter from China, and both my husband and I had job transitions. We had also moved homes (and cities!), started two of our three kids in new schools, completed three major surgeries, and were averaging six medical appointments a week. Life was a lot, laughter was sparse, and peace seemed just out of reach.

But in the midst of all that our family was navigating in that season, I still took comfort in an overall sense of order … that is, until my chest began to tighten, my breathing became shallow, and the undercurrents of what I later came to know as anxiety and mild panic took hold. These symptoms became an obvious sign that something was out of balance. Over time as I sought the Lord about each area and sat with a trusted counselor, my spiritual eyes were awakened that somehow, in the course of doing all that needed to be done, I had gotten off track internally. Not only had I misdirected the responsibility for all outcomes to myself and my ability to manage them, but also fear had taken root in my heart in several areas. As a result, I began to experience physical manifestations of a spiritual problem.

Have you ever been there? Many (if not most) of us have. Following the Last Supper as Jesus was preparing His disciples for what was to come, He addressed the issue of peace: "Peace I leave with you; my peace I give to you. Not as the world gives do I give to you. Let not your hearts be troubled, neither let them be afraid" (John 14:27 ESV). Our Lord Himself fully understood that we would face fear and troubled hearts, and in exchange, we would need His peace. And as we see all through Scripture, we have a choice to receive it. You see, what stands out to me in John 14:27 is not only that His peace is there but also that we have to take a step to gain victory. "Let not" is the admonition Jesus gives us. *Don't let* your heart be troubled. *Don't let* it be afraid. In our journey toward greater freedom in Christ, there is always a moment when we have to choose to make an active exchange—our life for His life. Our sin for His redemption. Our unforgiveness for His grace. Our fear for His peace.

Many times, when we're in some sort of turmoil, the easiest thing to do is stay there. There is something about our humanity that would prefer to sit in a pain that is comfortable than have the courage to ask God to take it away. During that season in 2018, I had choices to make. I had to choose if I was going to have the courage to make that active exchange. My fear for His peace. My desired outcome for His perfect plan. Sometimes the exchange of our life for His life—our pain for His healing—may come out as a bold declaration in prayer, and sometimes that exchange comes out as a whisper as we tenderly and carefully lay our deepest concerns before the Lord and wait for Him to meet them. But as we wait on Him and stay in His Presence, I have found that He always meets us there as our hearts are transformed.

PRAYER

Lord, I need You. There are areas of my life that are too much for me to carry. There are areas where fear has been the voice in my head, rather than the truth of Your Word. Lord, I make a choice today to exchange my fear for Your peace. I lay down my life in exchange for Yours. In Jesus' Name, Amen.

FOR FURTHER STUDY

John 15:4, 26, 33; Philippians 4:6–7; Colossians 3:15–16

FOR FURTHER REFLECTION

1. *Write down two areas that are troubling you. Ask the Lord to exchange your troubled heart for His peace.*

2. *Sit quietly for a few minutes in God's presence. As you present these things to Him, take a moment to hear from Him as you make the holy exchange.*

HOLY SPIRIT,
WHAT ARE YOU
SAYING TO
ME TODAY?

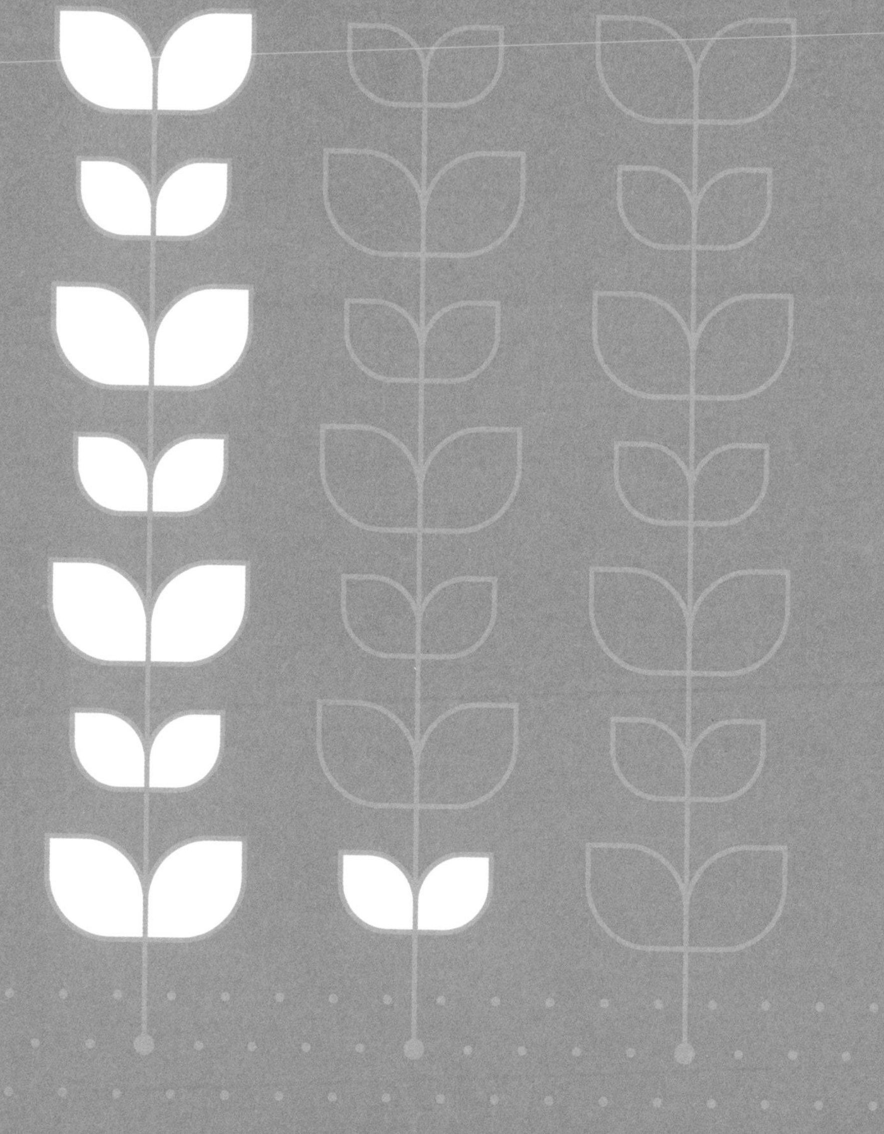

8

A Perfect Work

By Bridgette Morris

Count it all joy when you fall into various trials, knowing that the testing of your faith produces patience. But let patience have its perfect work, that you may be perfect and complete, lacking nothing.

JAMES 1:2-4

I love to garden. I like to grow things that are what I call "purposeful plants." Many beautiful flowers serve a purpose for sure, but my favorite plants actually produce something my family and I can eat. But the thing about gardening is that it's easy to grow impatient even though the end result is more than worth it.

For instance, I think we can all agree that peaches are delicious and juicy, right? And *especially* so when you get to pair a peach dessert with ice cream. (Who *wouldn't* enjoy that?!) I live near a grocery store, so even in the dead of winter, I can go buy a can of peaches and make a cobbler. There's a vast difference, though, in the quality of the peaches I *grow* versus the peaches I *find* on aisle three. That's why I choose to grow my own peaches—I know they're better for me, and they taste *much* better than peaches from a can.

But here's the thing: peaches take *time* to grow. If my end goal is a delicious, homemade cobbler made with fresh peaches and perfectly coupled with Blue Bell ice cream, then I have to take some steps before I can arrive there. First, I buy a peach tree and plant it. Then I water it, fertilize it, and make sure bugs don't infest it. After that, I prune the tree. All these steps happen *before* I see any fruit. I must be active in my waiting, or nothing will grow. I must be steadfast and have endurance to tend my garden before the fruit is even visible. If I don't, the fruit will never grow, and weeds will overtake the nutrition meant for the intended plant.

The first chapter of James opens with this charge, which is both encouraging and challenging: "Count it all joy when you fall into various trials, knowing that the testing of your faith produces patience. But let patience have its perfect work, that you may be perfect and complete, lacking nothing" (James 1:2–4). I would love to be that, wouldn't you? I mean, who doesn't want to be totally complete, lacking nothing? What catches my attention about this passage is the phrase "let patience have its perfect work." How does patience have work? As I investigated the original language, the word translated as patience in Greek is *hypomonē*, which means 'cheerful endurance, constancy, or patient continuance.' In the New Living Translation, it's translated as "endurance," and in the English Standard Version, it's translated as "steadfastness." What all these words have in common is the picture they paint—they showcase actions we take and how we can do our work. Patience can absolutely be waiting and stillness, but it can also be an act of continuing to walk out what has been laid before us for the purpose of refining and perfecting us.

Just like I do with my peach trees, if the goal in our lives is to be more Christlike—"perfect and complete, lacking nothing"—then we have to take intentional steps to get there, and one of those steps is allowing patience to have its perfect work in us. And sometimes patience looks more like consistency than stillness. I must be consistent to check on my garden while I wait for the fruit to grow. I must love my spouse consistently while we are both being transformed by the Holy Spirit. We need to be consistent with our children while they are growing into responsible adults, and we must consistently obey the Lord as He leads us into our destiny. Healthy marriages, loving parenting, and effective destinies don't happen overnight; they all require a steadfast consistency to see them come to fruition.

Letting patience have its perfect work in you requires being on God's timeline, not your own. "Active patience" is having an attitude of submission and gratitude for His timing instead of demanding God work on your timeline. Let's be consistent with what God has placed before us and patient with the trials we go through so that we can be transformed by the power of the Holy Spirit and showcase the goodness of God in the world around us.

PRAYER

God, thank You that the trials we face in our lives can be used by You to better equip us for our destinies. Today we choose to let patience have its perfecting work in our lives. Please give us wisdom on how to live patiently day after day as we seek to glorify You and see Your kingdom here on earth as it is in heaven. In Jesus' name, Amen.

FOR FURTHER STUDY

Colossians 3:12–13; James 5:7–8

FOR FURTHER REFLECTION

....

1. *How have past trials produced fruit you are currently enjoying in your life?*

2. *Ask the Holy Spirit to reveal any areas in which you need to let patience have its perfect work in your life.*

HOLY SPIRIT,
WHAT ARE YOU
SAYING TO
ME TODAY?

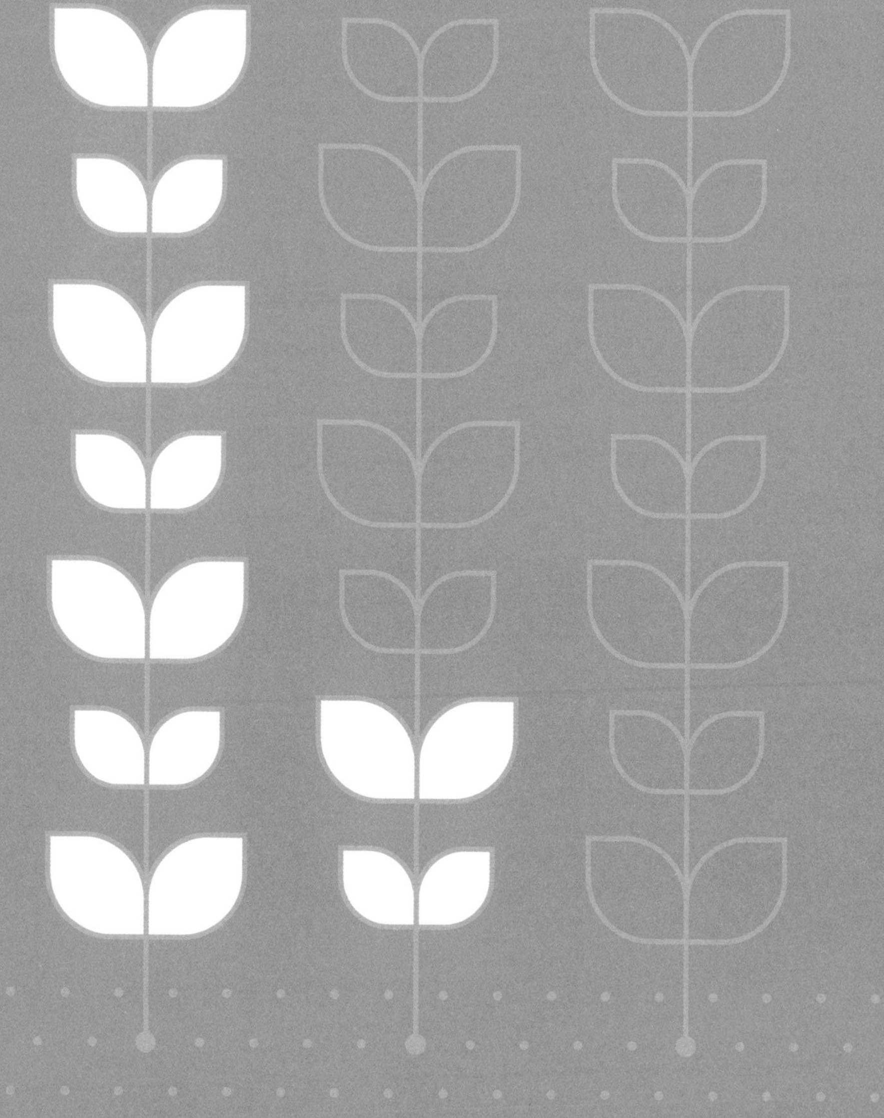

9

Are We There Yet?

By Sion Alford

But if we hope for what we do not see, we wait for it with patience.
ROMANS 8:25 ESV

When my wife and I lived in Florida, we would take our children to Walt Disney World every February. The trip took about six hours, and for the three young and energetic kids we had at the time, it felt like a lifetime. Very early in the trip, we'd hear their squeaky little voices from the back seat of our minivan ask, "Are we there yet?!" Every 15 minutes like clockwork, they'd ask again: "Are we there yet?"

As the journey went on, our kids grew anxious and became easily upset with each other. By the time we reached the halfway point of our trip, they were fighting over a toy from McDonald's. One was complaining that someone was touching him, and another was throwing French fries. What happened? They were tired of waiting and had lost their "patience." They had lost perspective.

How could this have possibly happened? Somewhere along the journey, they forgot something—they forgot they were going to Walt Disney World! They cared more about the temporary discomfort of cohabiting a minivan than they did about the amazing place they were going to visit. They wanted their current situation and circumstances to change immediately instead of recognizing that their temporary discomfort was for a purpose—to get them to their joyful destination!

The sound of their impatience escalated until what could be described as World War III broke out in the back seat. I did what all godly fathers do in situations like that—I calmly interrupted their childish tirades and said, "Dearest children, please refrain from your provocative attitudes of disruption and protestations of injustice and remain composed and collected until we reach our final destination." Ha! Not really! I actually grabbed the toy they were fighting over and yelled, "Whose toy is this?" "Mine!" cried two of the kids. Then, out of desperation, I held the toy out the car window (while going 70 miles per hour) and declared, "I am going to let this toy go if you guys don't quit fighting over it!" My young daughter began crying while my eldest son declared, "Let it go, Dad! Let it go!" I obviously knew to whom

the toy belonged, so I calmly returned it to my daughter.

Like any good pastor, I then took the opportunity to give a biblical life lesson about what just happened. I reminded them that God may allow us to experience difficult and uncomfortable situations on the way to our promised destinations. I also reminded them of the promise that was before us. I told them the journey was going to be worth the pain and temporary discomfort. We would get there. Magic Kingdom and Epcot were in their future. All they had to do to enjoy the trip was to embrace the journey and be patient.

Many people fail to realize that patience doesn't begin working in our hearts until we're irritated. Waiting for something and having patience are two different things. When we are waiting, we are simply pausing in expectation that the coming promise (answer to our prayers) is near and inevitable. Our waiting turns to patience when our expectations are not met, and our timing is violated. In other words, when we get tired of waiting, that's when patience begins!

There is a word for this process in the Bible: *suffering*. The apostle

Paul wrote, "We rejoice in our sufferings, knowing that suffering produces endurance [patience], and endurance [patience] produces character, and character produces hope" (Romans 5:3-4 ESV). Painful waiting (suffering) has the by-product of patience, and patience has the by-product of character.

Jesus lived this way. He experienced more suffering than any other person who has ever lived. The author of Hebrews wrote, "Keep your eyes on *Jesus,* who both began and finished this race we're in. Study how he did it. Because he never lost sight of where he was headed—that exhilarating finish in and with God—he could put up with anything along the way: Cross, shame, whatever. And now he's *there,* in the place of honor, right alongside God. When you find yourselves flagging in your faith, go over that story again, item by item, that long litany of hostility he plowed through. *That* will shoot adrenaline into your souls!" (Hebrews 12:1-3 MSG).

Jesus led the way for us. He plowed through the suffering. He knows that waiting will turn into patience, and patience will turn into character.

We *will* get there. The journey will be over one day, so maybe we can quit asking, "Are we there yet?" and start asking, "God, am I done yet?"

PRAYER

Father, I desperately need the patience Jesus had when He walked in Your perfect will. I depend on Your grace as I allow Your character to develop in my heart. The waiting may be difficult at times, but I choose to trust in Your unfailing love. You have good plans for my life, and the desire of my heart is to be with You always. In Jesus' name, Amen.

FOR FURTHER STUDY:

Romans 2:6–7; Luke 8:15;
Ecclesiastes 7:8;
2 Corinthians 6:4–6;
Galatians 5:22–23

1. What are some "journeys" God is taking you on? Do you find yourself asking Him, "Am I there yet?"

2. Think of a time where your waiting had to turn into patience. How did you handle it, and what character lessons did you learn from it?

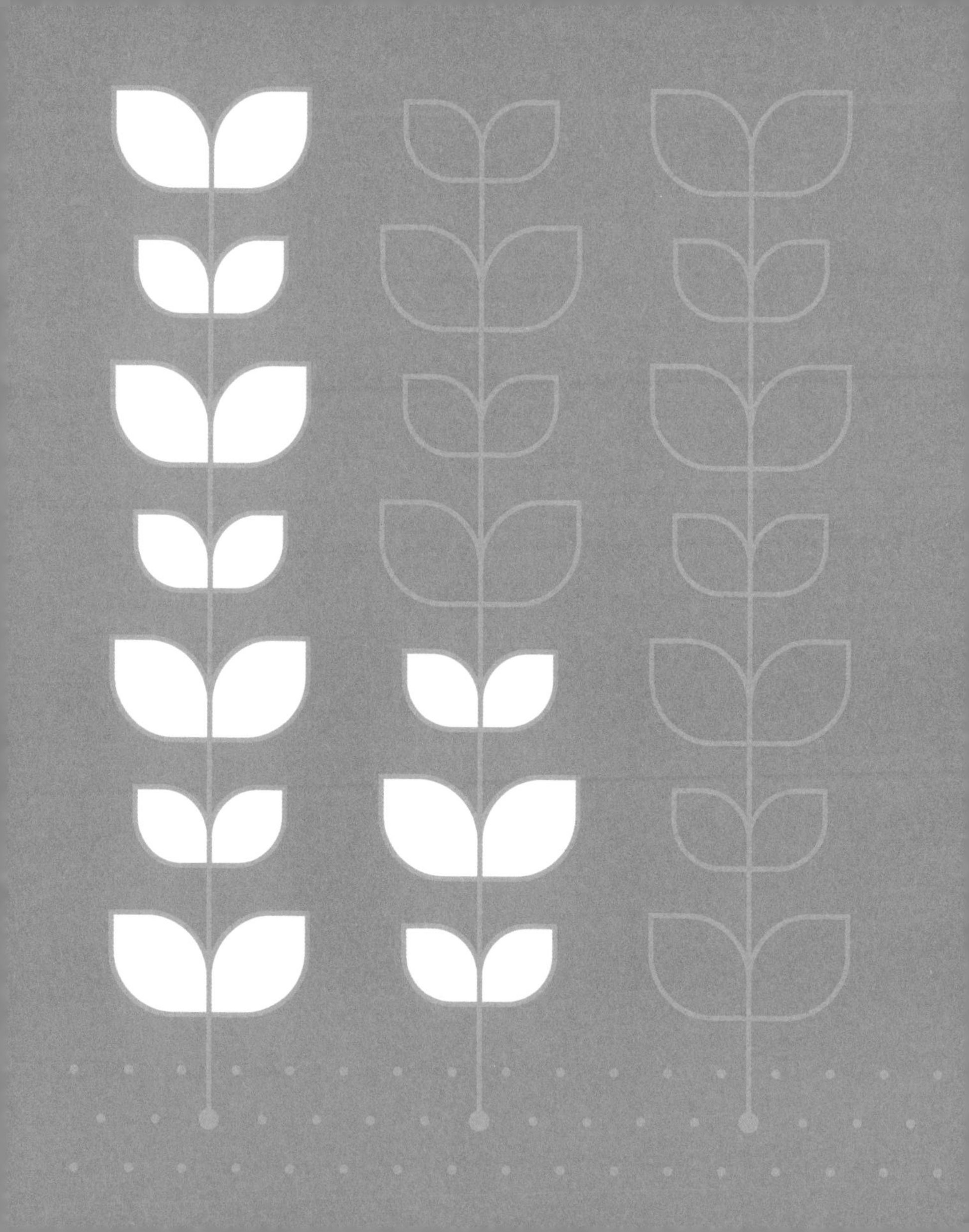

10

Be Kind, Be Intentional, and Repeat

By Monica Bates

Love endures with patience and serenity, love is kind and thoughtful, and is not jealous or envious; love does not brag and is not proud or arrogant.

1 CORINTHIANS 13:4 AMP

"Random acts of kindness" is a pop culture phrase intended to motivate us to be kind to one another. This idea got kickstarted in England in 1987, when Princess Diana shook the hand of a man who had AIDS, challenging the belief that the disease is transmittable by touch and showing unconditional love and kindness to a fellow human being. There are shirts, stickers, mugs, and bookmarks that represent this "movement," as well as a Random Acts of Kindness Day celebrated on February 17, which speaks volumes to the need and desire for kindness in our world today.

As great as that movement is, what I love about our God is that He is always *intentional*—He is never random. Kindness is a fruit of the Spirit He has given to help us walk in compassion and care for each other.

I remember a day when I was walking through a store, and a woman dropped some items she had in her hand. I rushed over to help her pick up the items and place them in her cart. She was very grateful, and I enjoyed the opportunity I had to lend the helping hand she needed at that time. Coming alongside someone to assist and give an encouraging word or just a smile is part of our role to play as children of God in our world today.

In the New Testament, kindness is translated from the Greek word *chrestotes,* which means 'the quality of being warmhearted, considerate, humane, gentle, and sympathetic.' It can also be described as a characteristic of true love as described in 1 Corinthians 13:4: "Love endures with patience and serenity, love is kind and thoughtful, and is not jealous or envious; love does not brag and is not proud or arrogant" (AMP).

An illustration of kindness in the Bible can be seen in the actions of the Roman centurion (officer) in Luke 7:2–6. The centurion had a servant who became ill, and the centurion did everything in his power to heal this servant. Now, the centurion could have used his resources in a different way, such as hiring a new servant. But kindness compelled him to use every resource at his disposal to help his servant find healing. When the centurion appealed to Jesus, the Lord could see his intentionality. Jesus knew the centurion was motivated by compassion and kindness, and He could feel his faith. Jesus spoke a healing word from a distance, and the centurion's servant was instantly made well.

How often do we see someone in need from a distance? How often do we hear the quiet voice of the Holy Spirit speak to our hearts to help someone with groceries, assist someone who is struggling, or speak a word of encouragement to someone who needs uplifting? As we act on what we hear and feel in these times, we are intentionally giving kindness to others. We are being the hands and feet of Jesus. Intentional kindness is the heart of God. Intentional kindness can—and will—change the world.

PRAYER

Father, please give you me Your eyes for those around me and help me see where I can show kindness today. Search my heart thoroughly, Father, and give me a heart of kindness. Highlight those around me who need a word of encouragement from You. Thank You, Lord, for Your intentional love toward me. Help me give what I have received from You to others and show me what intentional kindness looks like so I can love people well. In Jesus' name, Amen.

FOR FURTHER STUDY

Ephesians 4:32; Colossians 3:12; 2 Timothy 2:24; Philippians 2:4

FOR FURTHER REFLECTION

1. *Reflect on a time when someone was kind to you. How did it make you feel?*

2. *What would your life look like if you made the decision to walk in intentional kindness for 10 days in a row? Do you accept the challenge?*

HOLY SPIRIT,
WHAT ARE YOU
SAYING TO
ME TODAY?

11

The God Kind

By Thomas Miller

Because Your lovingkindness is better than life,
My lips shall praise You.

PSALM 63:3

I struggled to "get" it. It was just so difficult for me to understand. I *knew* it was true, but it was hard for me to *feel* like it was true.

You see, for several years of my life, from my late teens to my early 20s, I just didn't live for God. Although I grew up in church, I had chosen to walk away from what I knew to be right. My words, my actions, my thoughts—my life—were focused on *me*. Partying, promiscuity, and pretending were all parts of my day-to-day living.

But then God in His power and providence turned my life around. He stepped into the mess of my life and showered me with His kindness. I repented of my sins, wholeheartedly started following Him, and for the first time in my life had a deeply intimate, personal relationship with Jesus Christ. He loved me!

Yet I struggled to comprehend and fully receive it. God was so unrelentingly kind to me, but I didn't deserve it. It was difficult for me to look at the life

I had been living and feel like I could receive His kindness. It felt like I was taking something that didn't rightfully belong to me and that I didn't deserve. I was embarrassed by my past choices. How could God continue to be so kind to me when I had been so apathetic toward Him for so many years?

As I've continued to follow Him, though, God has time and time again showed me that this life I live is truly about the love relationship I have with Him—the love relationship that *starts* from Him. Who He says I am is who I am. I am not defined by my past; I am defined by His love for me. What a kind Father He is!

Even to this day, if I look at my daily mistakes, mess-ups, or missteps, it's easy to feel puzzled by God's kindness. Why would He still be so kind to me? Well, the truth is that His kindness is zero percent based on my failures and 100 percent based on His love for me. And that is true for you as well. His kindness toward you flows completely from His character, not from your flaws, faults, or failures. He is kind because of Who He is. His kindness is greater than, bigger than, and beyond any of our understanding. It's mysterious.

But it's real! We may not "get" it, but we get it. In other words, we may not fully understand it, but we are daily recipients of it. And it flows from Him in every season and every second, through the highs and the lows, the successes and the failures. Moment by moment, you can count on God's kindness.

In Psalm 63:3, David exclaims to God that His lovingkindness is better than life itself. How could *anything* be better than the precious gift of life? After all, if we don't have life, what do we have? But let me ask you this: what is life without the kindness of God? David knew that this life has true joy, meaning, and fulfillment only in God's kindness toward us.

So then the next question is this: since we've received such great kindnesses from God, how should we treat the people around us? There will definitely be times when others do things that annoy us, hurt us, or offend us. Their words and actions may even be malicious. So how should we respond? In those instances, the typical (and understandable) response is to either avoid, ignore in a passive-aggressive way, snap back, or retaliate. Those are all *natural* responses. But as followers of Jesus, we have His Spirit dwelling *in* us, and we're called to respond *supernaturally*—by showing kindness.

You might be thinking, *Wait, does this really apply to everyone? My family, my friends, and those I work with? What about those people I just casually meet throughout the day? Am I supposed to show kindness to every single person with whom I come in contact?* The answer is actually yes. I've discovered that when you show God's kindness throughout your daily life, it's like shining a light in the darkness. That warm glow of kindness stands in such stark contrast to what people experience in other parts of their lives. It's like a cup of cold water to the thirsty. Kindness is truly a gift. And it shines the light and love of God, even if people don't realize that it's God they are experiencing.

God's kindness flows directly from Who He is. It's not something He just shows on the outside yet in reality feels different on the inside—kindness is *fully* connected with Who He is. And His kindness can flow from His heart directly to you and then *through* you to others. It can be fully connected with how you feel on the inside and who you are as a person. The God kind of kindness always loves from the inside out. It is gracious to all and flows freely no matter how the other person acts. It is constant.

God's kindness is a gift you can give so many times throughout the day every day. Through your words and actions, your small, medium, and large acts of kindness can show God's love to so many. His type of kindness is better than life. And you get to give it to everyone!

Choose today and every day to give kindness—the God kind.

PRAYER

Father, Your kindness to me is better than life and anything else in this life. I ask You to live Your life through me so I can show Your kindness to everyone around me. In Jesus' name, Amen.

FOR FURTHER STUDY

Matthew 5:38–48; Psalm 25:6–7; Psalm 42:8; Psalm 143:8

1. *Reflect on the times when God has shown His amazing kindness toward you. How did His kindness change your heart?*

2. *Think about those who have offended you. Ask God to soften your heart toward them and show you ways to demonstrate kindness to them.*

HOLY SPIRIT,
WHAT ARE YOU
SAYING TO
ME TODAY?

12

Surprised By Kindness

By Kyle Fox

*Don't look out only for your own interests,
but take an interest in others, too.*

PHILIPPIANS 2:4 NLT

Personality assessments used to frustrate me, but I've grown to appreciate them as tools. They all classify me as an introvert, which is accurate but also a little humorous considering the stories I have that begin with the Lord prompting me to start conversations with strangers. My journal is full of these stories that would shock the professional who advised me to limit my interactions with people when I struggled with social anxiety years ago.

Nick wasn't expecting a guy visiting from Texas to awkwardly start a conversation with him while he was folding shirts at his retail job in a small mountain town. I remember telling myself how weird it was going to come across, but I *knew* I was supposed to talk to him. To my surprise, he responded by telling me he had recently surrendered his life to Jesus after moving across the country with initial plans to party and snowboard. We ended up grabbing coffee on his lunch break, where I learned of his desire for more Christian friends. That conversation alone made being brave and saying hello worth it, but it was just the beginning.

Several weeks after I returned home, Nick called me asking for help. He had followed through with plans to fly to Texas to visit someone but realized after arriving that he was about to put himself in a situation that wasn't good. He didn't know what to call it in that moment, but through kind, loving conviction, God spoke to his heart to protect him. Even though our homes were normally 13 hours apart, that particular day I was just 15 minutes away from where Nick needed to be picked up.

Some friends and I took Nick to lunch where we caught up before dropping him off at the airport for his new flight home. While we were in the car, Nick shared about all the Lord was doing in his life, including his upcoming first mission trip with his new church. Even though we didn't talk specifics, I could tell the thought of raising enough money to travel to Africa was daunting.

Early the next morning the Lord woke me up with a scripture to send to Nick and a burden to help with his mission funds. I'm pretty sure I prayed, "Surely this isn't You, Lord!" As a young adult at the time, the amount God put on my heart was the largest check I had ever written. I felt such an urgency to get it into Nick's hands that I had it overnighted to Colorado.

Not only was the Bible verse encouraging in Nick's season, but the check amount was exactly what he needed for his trip to be fully funded! But this whole story isn't at all about money—it's about a loving God letting Nick know that He saw him and was proud of him.

Nick and I remain close friends to this day, 15 years later. I have traveled across the country for his baptism. We've been in each other's weddings, and our families have become friends. Even students in our respective youth ministries have established life-giving relationships. We've never lived in the same state, and people have even pointed out how little we have in common. But relating to someone is less about sharing interests than it is about showing an interest in who they are.

This story isn't just about friendship. It's not about road trips, mission funds, or introverts being brave. Kindness is the thread woven through it all. When Nick tells the story, he speaks of my kindness. When I tell it, I highlight his. But after sharing this story for years, I've concluded that it's really about the Lord's kindness toward all of us. A kind God, who desires good things for His children, operates through us when we abide in Him.

Paul tells us to not only look out for our own interests but to also take an interest in others (see Philippians 2:4). Taking an interest in someone can radically alter the trajectory of their life, but it requires us to slow down, step out, and see past our differences. Quiet or outspoken, timid or brave, new believer or seasoned Christ-follower ... no matter your story, the Lord desires to show His kindness to someone through you.

1. When we acknowledge what hinders us, we're more likely to act in the moment. What insecurities do you face when you feel God nudging you to talk to someone?

2. Stepping out to show kindness to strangers can feel awkward and even scary. Relying on our feelings will hold us back, but relying on the God who fills us will move us forward every time. To whom is God asking you to show kindness today?

HOLY SPIRIT,
WHAT ARE YOU
SAYING TO
ME TODAY?

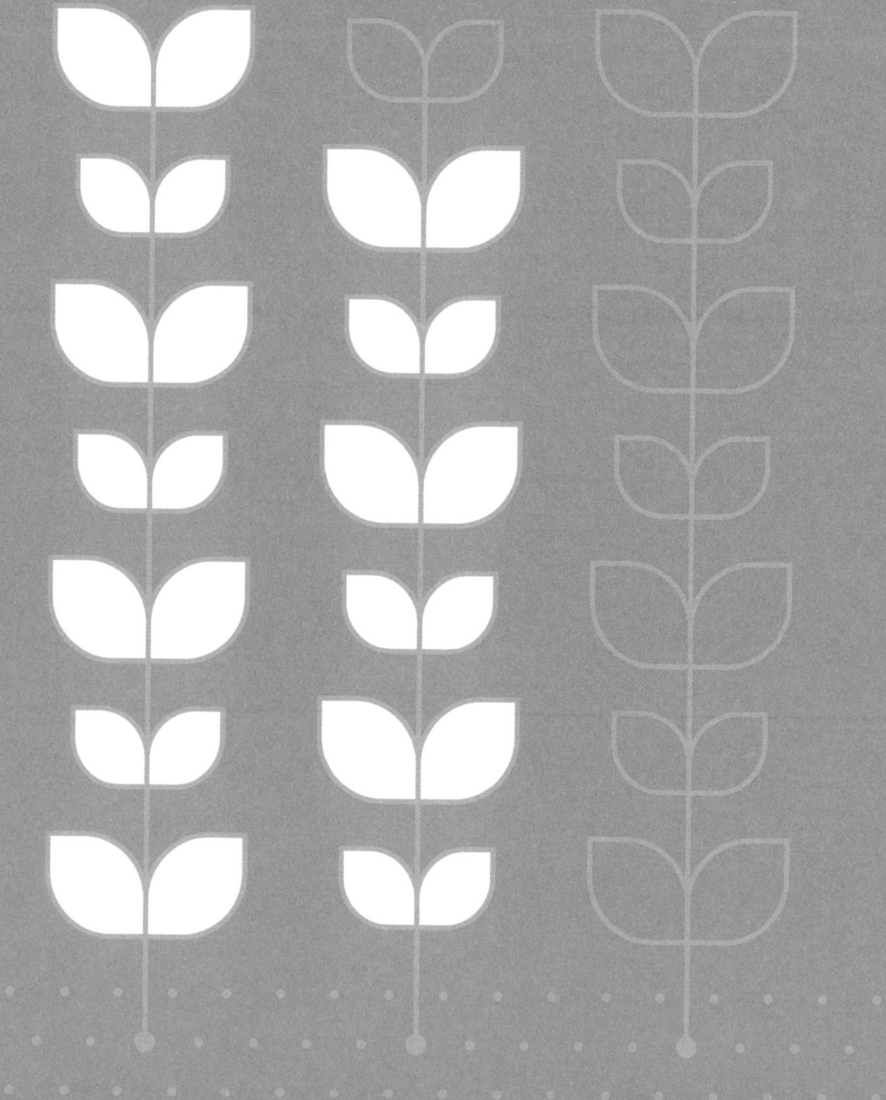

13

Now That's Good!

By James Morris

Beloved, do not imitate what is evil, but what is good. He who does good is of God, but he who does evil has not seen God.

3 JOHN 11

Imagine a par 3 on a golf course and hitting the ball within two feet of the hole. Someone might respond with "Good shot." Or being a baker and baking a delicious dessert. "Good cake" might be another appropriate response.

God created the earth, and He called it good. *Good*? I could come up with many unique words to refer to creation. It is incredible, phenomenal, exceptional, and so on. Ephesians 3:20 says God can do "exceedingly, abundantly above all we ask or think." I can imagine God's response after creating the earth being something more like, "Now *that* is exceedingly, abundantly above all that people could think or imagine." So why did He call creation *good*?

Jesus' first miracle was turning regular water into wine at a wedding, and it was called "the good wine" (John 2:10). The most extraordinary wine ever made was referred to as *good*. In the Gospels of Matthew, Mark, and Luke, Jesus is referred to as "Good Teacher," and in the Gospel of John, Jesus refers to Himself as "the Good Shepherd."

So what is *good*? Why is goodness, not greatness, a fruit of the Spirit? When God uses the term "good," He is referring to "that which God intends." For example, God called Creation "good" because it was as He intended. In fact, the first time God said something was *not* good was when man was alone. It is good for man and woman to be together because both are created in the image of God. Man alone was not the completion of what God intended, and therefore, it was not good. The full representation of God in male *and* female is good. God's intention was for a man to" "leave his father and mother and be joined to his wife, and they shall become one flesh" (Genesis 2:24).

Knowing that good is "that which God intends," we can grow in the fruit of the Spirit and be filled with goodness. If we experience goodness, we have a life of obeying God and fulfilling His will for our lives. At Gateway Church, we teach about hearing, believing, and obeying God. This is goodness. We can share God's goodness with others by being obedient and by being used by Him in all we do. It is God's intention for us to experience His kingdom here on earth.

First Peter 2:15-17 says, "For this is the will of God, that by doing good you may put to silence the ignorance of foolish men—as free, yet not using liberty as a cloak for vice, but as bond servants of God. Honor all *people*. Love the brotherhood. Fear God. Honor the king." The will of God is for us to do good. The way we do good is to do *that which God intends* for us. This Scripture passage explains that by doing that which God intends, we will "silence the ignorance of foolish men." In doing so, we will be bond servants of God and implement His intentions for us.

Because we are human, we need some general guidelines of what the will of God is. Start by honoring *everyone*—every age, gender, ethnicity, economic group, education level, etc. Honor all! Next, love your fellow Christ-followers and fear God. Finally, honor the authority and government under which you live. In doing these things, you are fulfilling the will of God.

Now, let's take it a step further. God has an individual calling for each of us. When you walk in His will, doing *that which God intends,* it is pure goodness. Of course, it doesn't mean everything is perfect every day, but it does mean that every day is *good.* We walk in our individual callings by hearing and obeying God.

Goodness is indeed a part of the fruit of the Spirit. Are we truly submitting our lives to be used in every moment by God? This is a life of submission to God and making Him Lord of every area. The more we do this, the more we experience the goodness of the fruit of the Spirit.

---

2 Matthew 19:16; Mark 10:17; Luke 18:18, all references NKJV

3 John 10:11, 14 NKJV

PRAYER

God, thank You for Your good creation. Thank You for Your good will for my life. Help me walk in daily obedience to You. I submit my life, schedule, words, and actions to Your will. Please speak to me every day and open my heart to hear Your voice. Give me the courage and boldness to follow Your direction and use me to make a difference for You. In Jesus' name, Amen.

FOR FURTHER STUDY

Matthew 7:17–18; Galatians 4:18; Ephesians 4:29; 1 Thessalonians 5:21

1. Read Matthew 5:16. How do your "good works" help others glorify God?

2. Is anything in your life not "that which God intends"? Ask the Lord what needs to change and what you need to do to bring about that change.

HOLY SPIRIT,
WHAT ARE YOU
SAYING TO
ME TODAY?

14

I Love You ... Be Good!

By Casey Hale

Imitate God, therefore, in everything you do,
because you are his dear children.

EPHESIANS 5:1 NLT

I recently had to have one of those "hard conversations" with my five-year-old. (Parents, you know exactly what I'm talking about!) I don't have any experience with parenting older kids, but I'd be willing to bet that discipline never gets easier. This particular conversation was about making better choices—choosing respect and obedience rather than consequences. Later on in that very same day, the Lord kindly sent me a corrective conversation through a fellow coworker, and I was gently reminded of the importance of my responsibility, both as a Christ-following mom and as a child of God. I had to ask myself, *Am I a living example of respect and obedience? Am I modeling the fruit of the Spirit for my children and others?*

Often, when we drop our kids off at school or leave them with a babysitter, my husband and I speak these parting words: "I love you ... be good!" While my hope is that my kids have seen goodness modeled in us and will choose to act "good," it's about so much more than behavior. The subtle implication of that short phrase is "remember our relationship—who you are—and act accordingly." As Christians, goodness is a posture of our heart, formed through our loving relationship with our heavenly Father. And out of that intimate relationship, our actions naturally overflow.

To develop an understanding of goodness as a fruit of the Spirit, we can first endeavor to define "goodness." The way the world defines goodness often fails to measure up to God's standard, so how do we know what is truly "good"? The Bible shows us the fruit of the Spirit in Galatians 5:22–23, and just a few verses earlier, Paul reminds the church that "the flesh desires what is against the Spirit" (Galatians 5:17 CSB). We must decide for ourselves if we are going to side with the world and our sinful human nature in what we think is good or with what the *Spirit* says is good.

This is quite often one of the biggest obstacles for anyone trying to understand the character of God. The all-too-common question is "If God is so good, why does He allow [fill in the blank]?" I've personally been there myself many times! It's happened most often for me in worship services, when we're singing about God's goodness. I can't help but think, *Things really don't feel good right now*. But we need to get to a place in our faith where our trust in God's goodness is stronger than our feelings or opinions of what *should* be good. God alone defines true goodness because *God is good*. When you start feeling that maybe your circumstances aren't so good, I encourage you to sing out in faith about God's goodness. You might not fully understand it in the moment, but we have the assurance of His Word to know that He is *always* good. He can't help it—that is just who He is.

If one of our foundational beliefs as Christians is that the Bible *is* truth, then we cannot ignore the evidence of God's good character written there. A simple Bible word search will list so many verses describing God's goodness. And because the Bible declares that God is good, we can then understand how *we* are to be good. We have a blueprint for what it looks like to display true, authentic goodness to others. What a gift!

Accepting salvation through Christ means we enter into a relationship with Him. Because God made Himself available to us through His Word and through prayer and conversation, we have immediate access to Him and His character. The more we get to know Him, the more we want to be *like* Him. Our made-new purpose becomes growing more and more into the image of Jesus with each passing day. And the evidence of our changed character is becoming a reflection of Jesus, which includes being a representation of the goodness of God here on earth to every person we interact with in our daily lives.

What a loving Father we have! He who is *good* in the purest, most true sense of the word *wants* to be in intimate relationship with *us*! He exemplifies goodness for us in every way and walks with us hand in hand as we learn to choose goodness in our everyday lives. "Acting good" is about pleasing others, but "being good" is about pleasing God. In addition, being good is accepting the truth of God's goodness and, because of our closeness with Him, reflecting that goodness to the world around us. Be encouraged today that God says to you, "Remember our relationship. Remember you are My child. Show My character to others. I love you … be good."

PRAYER

Dear God, thank You for loving me and wanting a relationship with me. Thank You for the transformative work of the Holy Spirit in my life. Thank You for walking hand in hand with me as I learn to navigate what it means to follow You, to be a reflection of You, and to become more and more like You. Help me to always remember that You are good and to choose goodness. In Jesus' name, Amen.

FOR FURTHER STUDY

Ephesians 2:8–10; Matthew 5:16; Ephesians 5:8–10; Ezekiel 36:27

1. Remember times in your life when the Lord has clearly revealed His goodness to you. How do those moments encourage you today?

2. If our actions were solely in response to what other people wanted from us or how they acted toward us, the world would be pure chaos! Think of a time when you reacted to a person or situation rather than choosing goodness. Talk with the Lord about it.

3. Receive God's grace today over previous times in your life where you moved without dependence on Him. Renew in your heart and mind a conscious effort to pursue and include Him in everything you do.

HOLY SPIRIT,
WHAT ARE YOU
SAYING TO
ME TODAY?

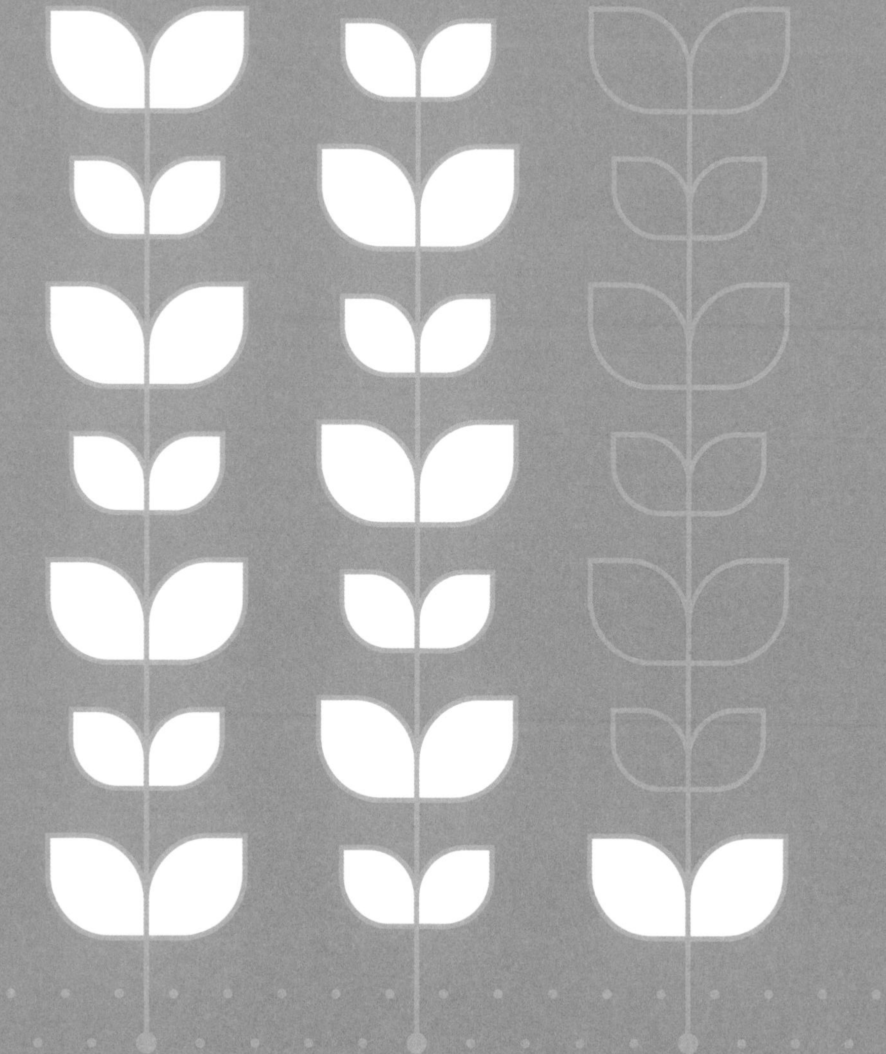

15

Rivers of Living Faithfulness

By Elizabeth Settle

Anyone who believes in me may come and drink! For the Scriptures declare, "Rivers of living water will flow from his heart." (When he said "living water," he was speaking of the Spirit, who would be given to everyone believing in him.)

JOHN 7:38-39 NLT

Our family of four uses a "chore cube" we created with one of our names written in bold Sharpie on each side: ELIZABETH, JASON, EMILY, ETHAN. When it's my turn to do the dishes, ELIZABETH stares at me from the cube on the counter. Once I empty the sink, I flip the cube, and now JASON takes his turn. It's a race in our house to turn your name as quickly as possible. Emptying a sink of one cereal bowl and spoon is much better than having to wash Seuss-style stacks of dirties piled to the brim.

My husband, Jason, and I have very different tolerance levels for a sink full of dirty dishes. I don't lose sleep waiting to wash them until morning, but my husband cannot understand this. If the cube displays ELIZABETH and Jason's anxiety wants the dishes done, he is free (and prone!) to wash them. But we have an agreement—he must wash them AS ME, not "for me." In other words, he does the deed, flips the cube, and the next name beams brilliant-as-the-sparkling-sink.

What's the difference between someone doing the dishes *for* me and someone doing the dishes *as* me? When the dishes are done *for* me, I wake up the next morning with the responsibility still screaming at me from the counter: ELIZABETH. When they are done *as* me, the work is finished. It's a full expression of generosity on Jason's part as he has borne the responsibility entirely on my behalf.

In 2 Corinthians 5:21, the apostle Paul tells us, "For God made Christ, who never sinned, to be the offering for our sin, so that we could be made right with God through Christ" (NLT). Jesus has borne the responsibility of sin entirely on our behalf. That truth displays God's faithfulness, which is a fruit of the Spirit. The strength of faithfulness is that its origin is in God. It's *His* faithfulness—not my own—that

sustains me. It's not that I am faithful to Jesus but that Jesus is entirely faithful to me. And He is entirely faithful to you. This is evidenced by His Spirit in us, pouring forth "rivers of living water" (John 7:38) that refresh our souls.

What an invitation! To relax upon the "rivers of living water" is to rest from our work and yet still be moving. We are progressing by the river's power. Faithfulness, then, is the substance upon which we rest (see Hebrews 11:1). Jesus' faithful work on the cross made us alive together with Him (see Colossians 2:13). His faithfulness freed us from sin and made us children of God! It's in being who we are—God's children—that we reflect our Father's faithful nature.

What about the responsibilities of life that rush all around? Chores for ELIZABETH still reverberate from the kitchen counter. I relate to Martha who had her own sink full of dirty dishes to clean. Jesus said, "Martha, Martha, you are worried and troubled about many things" (Luke 10:41 NKJV). On the other hand, her sister Mary was praised for choosing the good part— the sitting-at-Jesus'-feet part. The good news is the Spirit's indwelling empowers us to be Mary and Martha at the same time.

Jesus said, "It is best for you that I go away, because if I don't, the Advocate (the Spirit) won't come. If I do go away, then I will send Him to you" (John 16:7 NLT). Jesus baptizes us with His Spirit, gracing us with the ability to sit at His feet while we wash the dishes! Both are possible because "I have been crucified with Christ; it is no longer I who live, but Christ lives in me; and the *life* which I now live in the flesh I live by faith in the Son of God, who loved me" (Galatians 2:20). Our union with Jesus enables us to work faithfully while also resting in His faithful work! *This* is the power of relaxing in the river of living faithfulness that is His Spirit in and through us.

Thank You for Your faithfulness, Jesus. You are the strong and dependable One in this relationship! Holy Spirit, please remind me of God's faithful love. I choose to relax in receiving the Spirit that You pour into me and through me. Thank You that I am empowered to progress in life by the current of Your living water. In relaxing, I worship You. I trust You! I sit at Your feet and behold You, even as I meet the demands of life. In Jesus' name, Amen.

FOR FURTHER STUDY

2 Corinthians 5:21; Colossians 2:13; Galatians 2:20

1. Spend some time purposely relaxing. Get comfortable. Set your head back on the couch. Turn the eyes of your heart to God. Ask Jesus to pour His Spirit into and through you like living water. As you breathe, rest in the reality of His power carrying you. What does the Holy Spirit want to say to you about this?

2. What responsibilities worry and trouble you? Decide to approach those demands with a heart turned toward Jesus. Choose to worship God by "sitting at His feet" as you do your work. In what way does this inner awareness change the burden of the job?

HOLY SPIRIT,
WHAT ARE YOU
SAYING TO
ME TODAY?

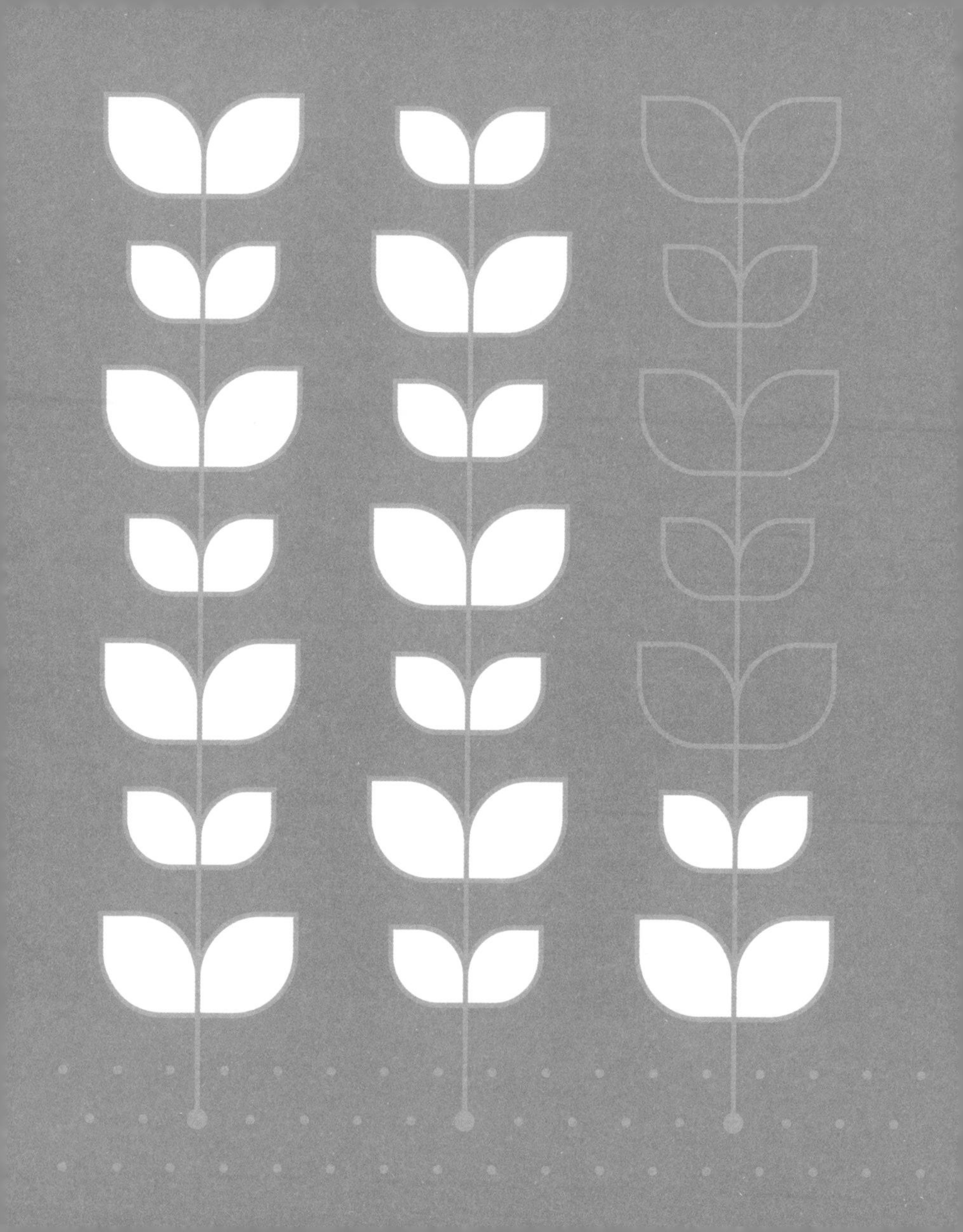

16

A Slippery Slope

By Tom Lane

For the word of the Lord is upright,
and all his work is done in faithfulness.

PSALM 33:4 ESV

A number of years ago, my wife, Jan, and I were leaders for a young adult ski trip in Colorado. We had about 50 young adults to watch over and care for, and we wanted to do some skiing as well. It never occurred to me to consider which activity was the higher priority. My default attitude was that I could fulfill my responsibility to lead the group and at the same time enjoy some really great skiing. These two issues—one an opportunity and the other a responsibility—didn't present any conflict of interest in my mind.

On the first day of the trip, we all trooped into the ski shop to pick up our rental skis and boots. It just so happened that I was one of the first to get everything on, which was great because I was ready and anxious to hit the slopes. It didn't occur to me to stay back and fulfill my responsibility as a leader to make sure everyone else got skis and boots that properly fit. After all, they were adults! My sole focus was on the opportunity before me. As far as I was concerned, it was every man and woman for themselves, and the last one to the slopes was a rotten egg.

As Jan and I headed out to the lift, one of the leaders asked if we would wait for her so she could ski with us. We quickly agreed and said we'd wait for her at the lift. But then we waited for what seemed to be *forever*. I started to get impatient because she'd been right behind us, and I couldn't imagine what was taking her so long. People were streaming into the lift line, and we were missing precious slope time! After waiting for a seeming eternity (even though it was probably only five to ten minutes), I assumed something had changed with our friend, and Jan and I joined the lift line to head up the mountain.

We made several runs down the slope and never caught up with the leader who wanted to ski with us. Later, when we came in for lunch, the leader confronted us. She was hurt and offended by our unfaithfulness to keep our word to wait and ski with her, and she wondered how we could be so casual with our commitments. She wanted an explanation for the disconnect and asked, "Aren't you supposed to demonstrate faithfulness as a leader?"

It was difficult to stop myself from becoming defensive. I wanted to explain my reasoning, but the reality was I was wrong. This situation had exposed in me an unfaithfulness to my word, and I needed to acknowledge it and repent.

That situation was a hard and embarrassing lesson, and since then, I've come to understand that faithfulness is one of God's most important characteristics. The truth is, I enjoy and experience God's faithfulness every day. Lamentations 3:22–23 says, "The steadfast love of the Lord never ceases; his mercies never come to an end; they are new every morning; great is your faithfulness" (ESV).

Being faithful means we are **steadfast in affection or allegiance** and loyal as a friend. It means we are conscientious and firm in our adherence to promises and responsibilities, both at home and at work. Therefore, we live true to our promises and do not embellish the facts or ignore or defend our mistakes.

Faithfulness is a fruit of the Spirit. In other words, the Holy Spirit's work in our life produces faithfulness in us. Now, I had a choice on the ski trip. I could explain away my unfaithfulness as being just a minor or even trivial error or misunderstanding and then dismiss it as "not a big deal." Or I could see it as a character flaw with big consequences impacting those I love and care for as a leader. Proverbs 20:6 describes this well; it says, "Many a man proclaims his own steadfast love, but a faithful man who can find?" (ESV).

What areas of your life need shoring up? Faithfulness comes from **a place of trust and loyalty**. As a follower of Christ, it is important that we are faithful to God. It is one thing to simply believe in Him but another to be faithful to Him. And our faithfulness is expressed in the way we treat and respond to others.

If any area of your life has even a single seed of unfaithfulness, please don't dismiss it. Instead, confess it, apologize for it, and let God develop the fruit of faithfulness in your life.

PRAYER

Lord, thank You for Your steadfast love and faithfulness to me. I ask You to develop the fruit of Your character in me so that I might reflect Your faithfulness in all my ways. In Jesus' name, Amen.

FOR FURTHER STUDY

Psalm 25:8–10; Numbers 23:19; Psalm 119:89–90

FOR FURTHER REFLECTION

1. *Think about a time when God demonstrated His faithfulness to you. How did it change your circumstance or perspective?*

2. *Allow the Holy Spirit to remind you of any situation in which you were unfaithful to your word recently and ask Him to show you how to make it right. This correction may involve humbling words or actions (or even both), but you will never regret being obedient to God's voice.*

HOLY SPIRIT,
WHAT ARE YOU
SAYING TO
ME TODAY?

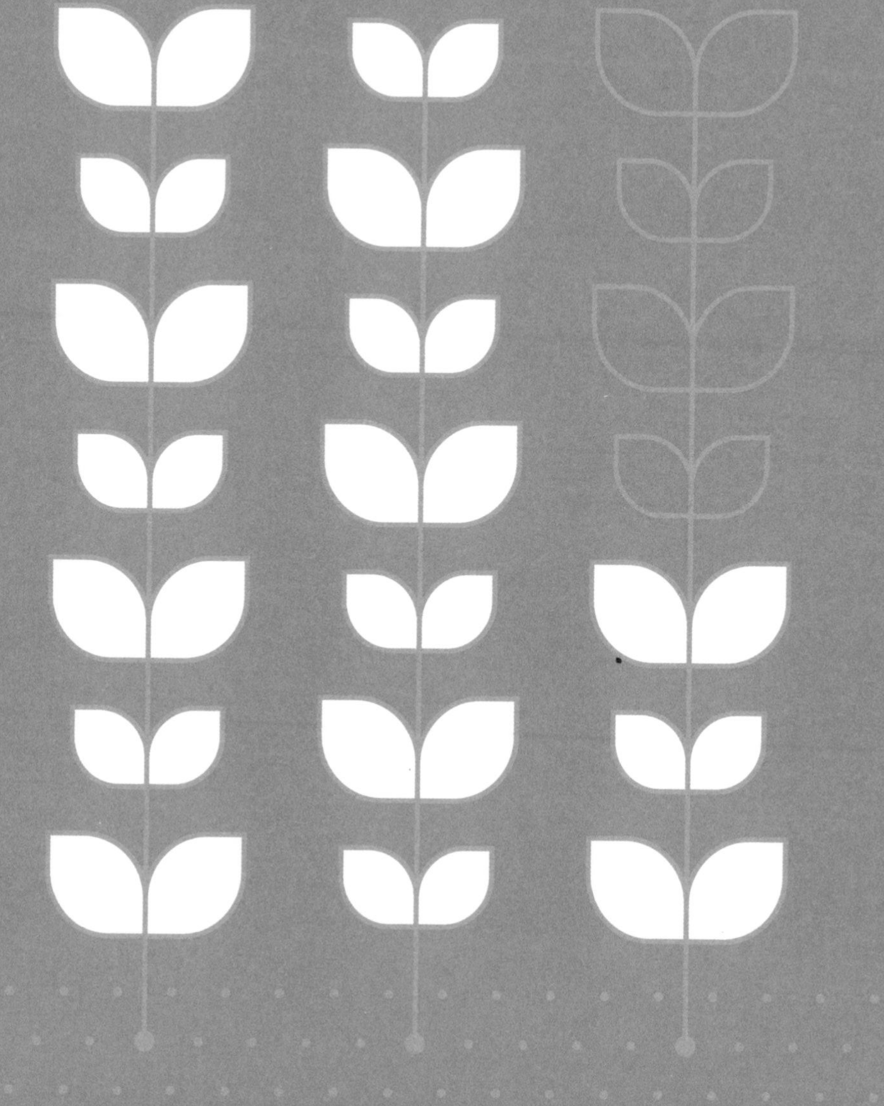

17

Giving Up My Right to Be Right

By Dr. Irini Fambro

But what happens when we live God's way? He brings gifts into our lives, much the same way that fruit appears in an orchard—things like affection for others, exuberance about life, serenity. We develop a willingness to stick with things, a sense of compassion in the heart, and a conviction that a basic holiness permeates things and people. We find ourselves involved in loyal commitments, not needing to force our way in life, able to marshal and direct our energies wisely.

GALATIANS 5:22-23 MSG

I like being right. I mean, who can honestly say they *enjoy* being wrong? I like having the right answers to a question, an equation, a good place to eat, a puzzle ... you name it. The only problem is that it has trained my ear to listen for what I am against, what I don't agree with, and what I think is wrong. This mental framework makes every conversation a lot of work. I am constantly analyzing, comparing, contrasting, evaluating, and overthinking what people are saying. What ensues are conversations that produce the kind of fruit that Paul listed *before* the fruit of the Spirit: "hostility, quarreling, jealousy, outbursts of anger, selfish ambition, dissension, division" (Galatians 5:19-20 NLT). Of course, I don't name the fruit of those conversations in that way, because I justify them in a more eloquent way. I am not hostile; I am Egyptian, and we are just a passionate people. I am not quarreling; I'm simply offering another perspective. I'm not jealous; I'm just observing someone's life. I'm not angry—again, I already told you I am passionate! I am not selfish; I talk about other people all the time. I am not creating dissension; I'm just being discerning. I am definitely not divisive; I just have my own opinion.

Is that too much honesty? Can I give space for each of us to be real about the struggle to be human? The unappealing fruit Paul listed is what stems from a life that "develops out of trying to get your own way all the time" (Galatians 5:19 MSG). Ugh! Here I am, where I started, with the desire to be *right*, which is really a disguise for getting my way all the time. Maybe I do have a part to own in all the hostility, quarreling, jealousy, anger, selfishness, dissension, and division around me. Have I sown seeds through my thoughts, words, silence, facial expressions, side-texts, and actions that produce the wrong fruit around me?

The reality is that I would have to answer "yes" (insert mourning face emoji here). If you share in this honest confession, then Paul wants to offer us hope today. There is another seed we can sow. There is another life offered to each of us. God offers freedom that can release each of us from the enslaving life our humanity creates. Life in partnership with the Holy Spirit gives us the opportunity to produce the fruit of the Spirit: "love, joy, peace, patience, kindness, goodness, faithfulness, gentleness, and self-control" (Galatians 5:22–23 NLT). This is the fruit I desire to produce. This is where I want to get it right.

Now, the fruit of the Spirit is not supposed to be seen as an à la carte selection—"I will take love, joy, and peace, but I am highly allergic to patience and gentleness." I know, it would be better if it could just stay as a nice thought or a great idea. Yet the Holy Spirit wants me to know that this fruit applies to my life, to your life, and to the lives of the people around us. Now it's personal, which is another way of saying that it's harder, messier, and crunchier, because people are involved. I wouldn't be hostile, jealous, angry, selfish, or divisive if people weren't in the equation. I really wish I had something to help me with people.

Insert gentleness. I know, not the fruit I would have seen as the solution, yet it is precisely what our world is missing and even craving. Gentleness is a strength, not a weakness; it is active, not passive. Gentleness cares more about people than about being right. Gentleness changes *how* I say what I'm thinking. Gentleness shifts *how* I listen to those around me. What if through gentleness I trained my ear to listen for something different? How can I take care of people's hearts? What pain might have brought them to their passionate opinion? In what areas do we have common ground?

In our world we are surrounded by the fruits of hostility, quarreling, jealousy, anger, selfish ambition, dissension, and division. Could it be that we are placed in a specific place for a specific time, with specific people, for a specific conversation so that we can gently take care of people's hearts and hurts?

PRAYER

Father God, thank You for not leaving us in the hostile, jealous, angry, selfish, and divisive environments that our human nature so easily creates. Give us the courage to own our part in those environments. Thank You, Holy Spirit, for your gentleness with our own hearts and hurts. Your gentleness tenderly shows us how to nourish people's hearts and hurts and offer the healing only You can bring. In Jesus' name, Amen.

FOR FURTHER STUDY

Proverbs 15:1; 1 Peter 3:15; Colossians 3:12; Philippians 4:4–5

In your next conversation, ask yourself the following questions:

1. *How can I take care of this person's heart?*

2. *What pain might have brought them to their passionate opinion?*

3. *What areas do we have in common?*

HOLY SPIRIT,
WHAT ARE YOU
SAYING TO
ME TODAY?

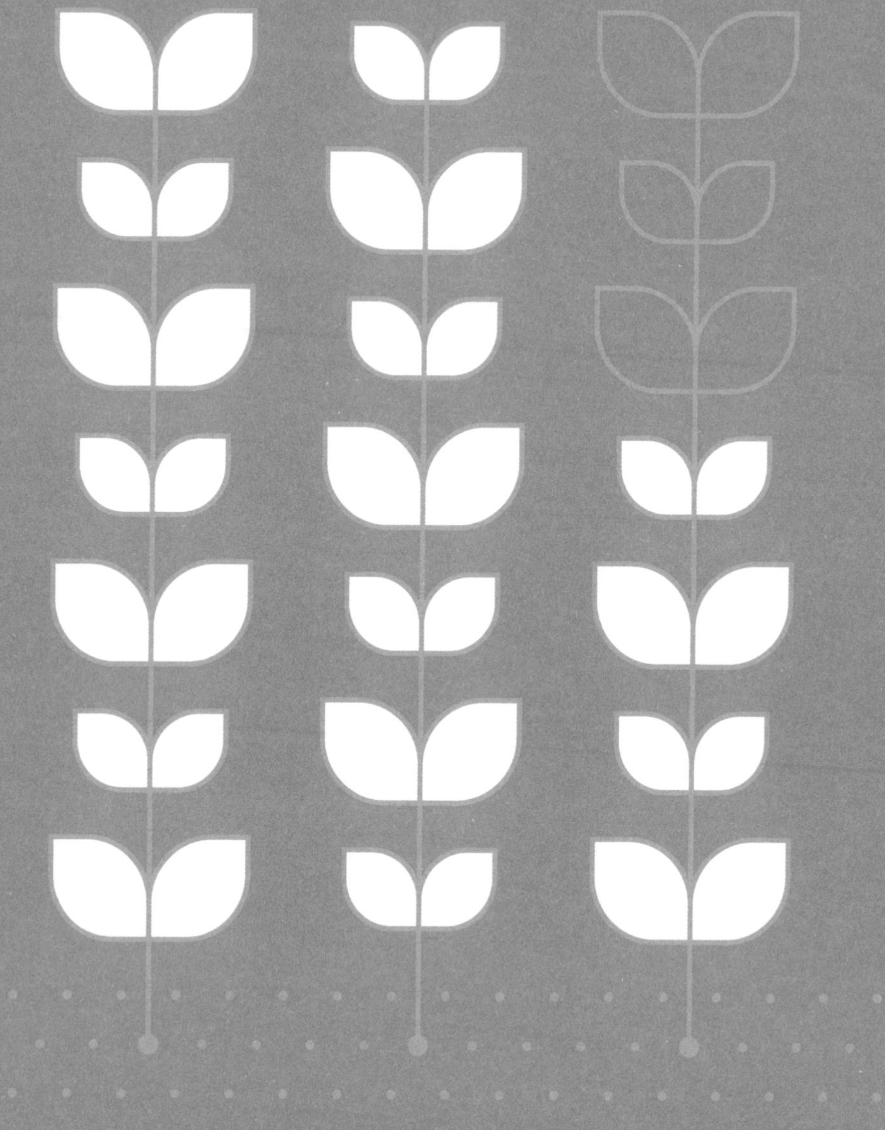

18

The Way of the King

By Todd Lane

Say to Daughter Zion, "See, your king comes to you, gentle and riding on a donkey, and on a colt, the foal of a donkey."
MATTHEW 21:5 NIV

Growing up, I loved watching wrestling—no, not the legitimate kind but the one you watched at an event called "Wrestlemania" with guys like Hulk Hogan and Macho Man Randy Savage. There was also a cartoon on Saturday mornings that made these characters even more grandiose in my mind! They were arrogant, tough, and brash with the kind of charisma that demanded attention. These wrestling matches and often all-out brawls played out without a single drop of blood. Amazing. What a show. What a facade.

Like everything the enemy has done to pollute our world, this is a perverted image. While those guys were physically strong, that's about the only thing that was true to form. Most everything else about their image was manufactured and fake. Their taunting was rehearsed. Their outcomes were predetermined. Their fights were choreographed. All in all, it was a hollow show. I'm sure for most of you I didn't need to go into this level of critique to convince you that professional wrestling is a farce! But it provides such a great parallel to how the ways of this world lead only to disappointing disillusionment. Those WWE wrestlers have more in common with Goliath than any other biblical figure, and we all know he was taken down by a lowly shepherd boy. So why does our society continue to celebrate the same traits of arrogance and brashness in our leaders?

God has a different way. The way of our King is gentle. In His sovereignty, He is not demanding or tough. In fact, His lordship is all about giving us a choice to love Him. When God sent His Son to the world, we received the truest human image of God's intentions. Humanity had *Emmanuel*—"God with us."

God didn't send His Son, Jesus, into the world so that He would condemn us but instead so that we would be saved through Him (John 3:17). Certainly, that salvation is from eternal death and separation from God, but He *also* saved us from being enslaved by human depravity here on earth. He has given each of us a new image and way by which to live our lives. Jesus spent a lot of time talking about His style, which He described in an over-arching theme of gentleness (meekness in Matthew 11:29; servanthood in Mark 10:45; humility in Matthew 25:40; peace in John 14:27). Jesus' kingly entry into Jerusalem, as described in Matthew 21:5, was prophesied in Zechariah 9:9 as "lowly and riding on a donkey" (NIV).

It doesn't take much study of history to know that kings as a general rule were not at all gentle. In fact, most kings were like those WWE wrestlers—arrogant, tough, and brash. To conquer land and establish kingdoms, that was the way it had to be done. Even Jesus' disciples expected Him to establish His kingdom by conquering, and Jesus continually had to show them a different way. His way broke from conventional thought, which left the disciples declaring, "This is a hard teaching" (John 6:60 NIV). They didn't understand! How could gentleness be the way to establish a kingdom? And while it wasn't a way to establish an *earthly* kingdom, it was the way to bring the kingdom of heaven to earth.

Jesus entered this earthly realm from a spiritual realm and brought with Him kingdom principles that turned the world upside down.

Jesus calls Himself the Good Shepherd (John 10:11), and this kingly image of a shepherd also connects to David, who was picked by God to go from shepherding his father's herd to shepherding the nation of Israel. We know shepherding requires strength because David said he had to physically fight off a lion and a bear. And after declaring that He is the Good Shepherd, Jesus went on to say it was because a good shepherd lays down his life for his sheep. This shepherding sure is a risky business! Still, shepherds are not known to be strong and powerful with the sheep. They do not *drive* the sheep; they *guide* them with gentleness. The combination of strength and gentleness displayed by a shepherd is the imagery Jesus modeled for us.

Our human nature is at war with the things of the Spirit. That is why we need the Holy Spirit to fill us to be empowered to walk this life. Jesus said that you will know people by their fruit (see Matthew 7:16), so calling character traits "fruit" is meaningful.

The world will know if we are being guided by the Holy Spirit when they see His fruit in our lives, especially because gentleness is in stark contrast to what the world offers. Filled with the Holy Spirit, followers of Jesus have an incredible opportunity to testify of our King. His gentleness is His strength. Let's show them the way of the King!

PRAYER

God, we know we battle against spiritual forces of darkness, but You are greater! We can take courage because You have overcome the world, and we receive your Holy Spirit to guide us into this day. May we bear the fruit of Your kingdom and reflect You, our King, so others will want to know You.
In Jesus' name, Amen.

FOR FURTHER STUDY

John 10:1–18; John 14:25–31;
Zechariah 9:9–13

1. *What does gentleness mean to you? Do you see it as a sign of weakness or strength? Why?*

2. *Ask the Holy Spirit to show you a way you can be gentler toward someone today.*

HOLY SPIRIT,
WHAT ARE YOU
SAYING TO
ME TODAY?

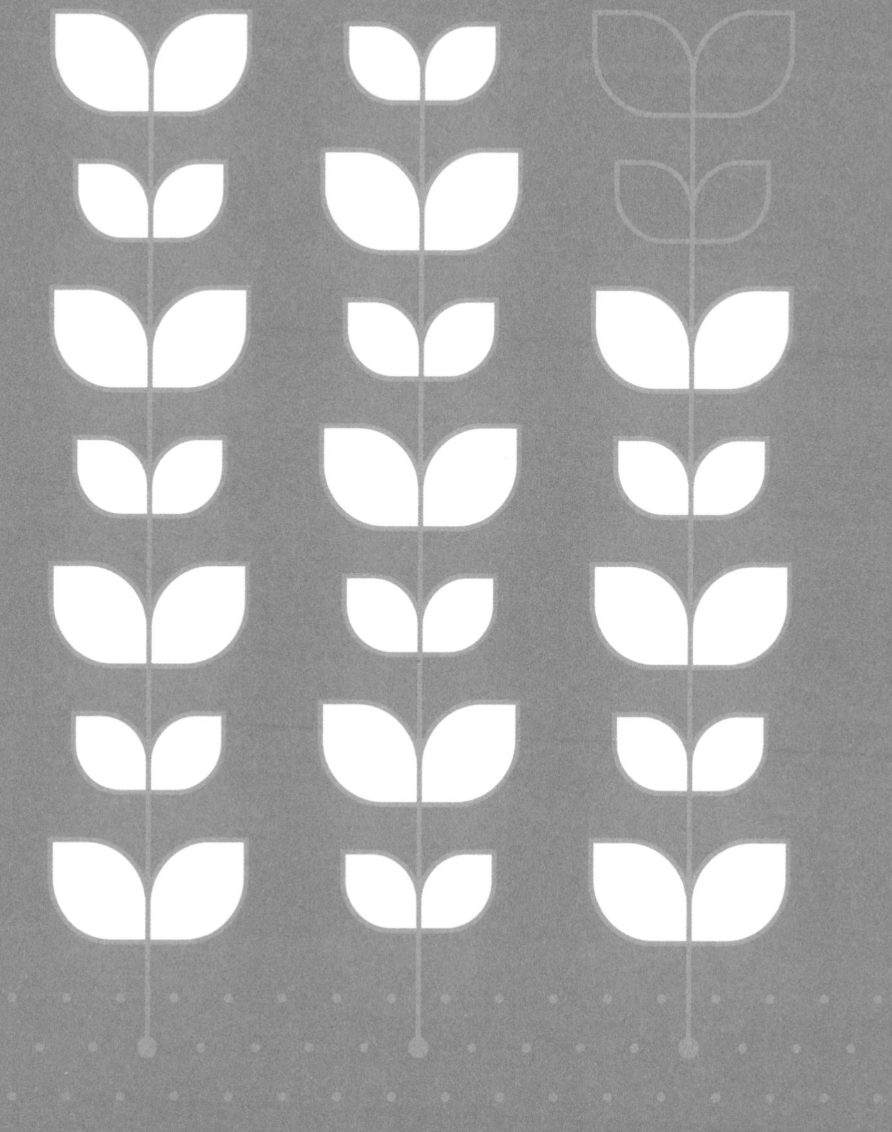

19

Lay Down Your "Self"

By Chelsea Seaton

Then he said to the crowd, "If any of you wants to be my follower, you must give up your own way, take up your cross daily, and follow me. If you try to hang on to your life, you will lose it. But if you give up your life for my sake, you will save it."

LUKE 9:23-24 NLT

"Oh, wonderful, we finally made it to the self-control fruit." [Insert eye roll here.] "Get ready for the pastor to yell at us about how we need to stop doing bad things and have more control over our temptations." I'm sure that's what you're thinking or nervous about me doing. Don't worry; that's not what this devotional is about. When I was assigned the task of writing about the fruit of self-control, I rolled my eyes and thought, *They have the wrong person. I'm not the one who needs to be writing about this.* I thought of all the perfect pastors I serve with who would be much better suited to give you an encouraging word that would inspire you (and me) to have more self-control. But alas, I said yes, and here we are.

As I prayed and wrestled with God, He showed me something I've never seen. Probably like most of you, I viewed this fruit as the ability to stop doing bad things. When I mess up, my first thought is, *Why couldn't I have more self-control*? When I'm aggressively driving down the highway 20 miles per hour over the speed limit, weaving between the cars who are in my way, why can't I just have more self-control? (That's a hypothetical situation, of course. I would never drive like that, but I think others do.)

But what if having self-control isn't about mustering up the willpower to avoid doing bad things until you either eventually give in or you feel really good about avoiding-self, resulting in pride? What if having self-control is all about giving up control of your "self" to someone else? Pastor Robert often asks, "Have you given control of your life to Jesus?" Giving up control is not something we do only at the moment of salvation. It is a daily practice of saying to Jesus, "My life is not my own. I give You control today."

We often view self-control as the ability to avoid bad things and do good things. Avoid the cookies in the break room and do the workout. Avoid embellishing and do tell the truth. Avoid driving like a maniac and do calm down! (That one is for me.) Those are great things, but if you're trying to do or not do by your own willpower, then you will eventually grow tired and frustrated. Why? Because there is no life in behavior modification. Behavior modification always leads to condemnation when we fail and pride when we succeed. True, authentic life is found by being in relationship with Jesus.

Like any relationship, the closer you become, the more you start to act like the other person. You start to say things at the same time, or you leave the house in matching clothes without planning on it. It's the same with Jesus—the more we enter into relationship by spending time with Him, the more we begin to desire what He desires, love what He loves, and follow His way of living.

Now, like any relationship, it's not always easy. Some days it takes a lot to lay ourselves down and submit to another. It's the same with Jesus. We can be under attack or just having one of those days, and we need to lay ourselves down again at the feet of Jesus. We need to pick up His cross and follow Him. When we give up ourselves to the control of Jesus, the result is always life.

I am convinced the way to bearing more self-control fruit in our lives is not in rallying our willpower but through simply staying connected in relationship. When we focus on our life-giving relationship with Jesus over willpower, we will experience His joy and freedom. Sometimes relationship will say, "Eat the cookie," and that's not wrong—Jesus loves a celebration. Perhaps the relationship says, "Tell the truth" because the story is hilarious and Jesus loves to laugh. The relationship might even say, "Skip the workout because I created your body, and it needs to rest today." Life-giving relationship will say, "My way is peace, and I want you to have peace and create peace on the highway." It is by the power of the Holy Spirit and by giving up control of our "self" to Jesus that we find true self-control.

Today, let's not focus on having more self-control to behave the right way. Let's tell Jesus, "I give You control of myself today. Through our relationship, may Your life be in me, and may I follow Your ways."

PRAYER

Jesus, today I lay down my selfish ways to follow You. Please forgive me for the times my life hasn't reflected my relationship with You. Thank You that according to Your Word, when we give up our lives, we find new life in You. Please fill us fresh today with Your life and power.

FOR FURTHER STUDY

Hebrews 4:15–16; 1 Peter 4:7; Matthew 16:24-26

1. Reflect on how you view self-control. Is it life-giving or not? If it brings feelings or thoughts of shame, ask Jesus to show you how He sees you.

2. Are there areas where your life isn't reflecting that you've given Jesus control? What would it look like for Him to lead you into new life?

HOLY SPIRIT,
WHAT ARE YOU
SAYING TO
ME TODAY?

20

Not the Most Popular Fruit

By Elisabeth Dunn

*A man without self-control is like a city broken into
and left without walls.*

PROVERBS 25:28 ESV

As a child, learning to read was a struggle. But after lots of tears (mine) and multiple prayers (my mom's), I became a voracious reader. I love the written word. If I had to lose one of my five senses, I would give up hearing. I could live in a silent world, but I could not live without the written word. Reading has made my world big and wonderful. Reading is how I learned about Amy Carmichael as a teenager and knew

I wanted to visit India one day. And then in 2014, I had the privilege of spending two months in India. Through books, I was introduced to the great Russian Empire of the 1800s, and later getting to experience the places I had read about in person was one of the most extraordinary events in my life. I learned about people who became heroes to me, like Anne Frank (I may or may not have also given my diary a name as a teenager), Corrie Ten Boom, and Virginia Hall, just to name a few.

I don't reread books often, but I do read the Bible in its entirety almost every year. The Bible is like no other book ever written, and it is by far the most important book I read because it is living and active (see Hebrews 4:12). And as a teenager, I always tried to read my Bible before I read any other book.

As I grew older, though, and everything I read wasn't chosen by my parents or a teacher, I had to learn that what I let through my eye-gate wasn't only about the movies or shows I watched; it *also* related to what I let in through reading. I didn't always do the best in this area. One day in my early 20s, I felt a prompting from the Holy Spirit that I needed to fast a particular genre of literature for a year.

I don't talk about this a lot because it's kind of embarrassing to tell people I fasted romance books for a year. Now before you get all judgy, I wasn't reading those romance books with shirtless men on the front. Just your good ol' run-of-the-mill Christian romance. A little Janette Oke here, some Lori Wick there, and a sprinkle of Francine Rivers everywhere.

The books I was reading weren't bad; in fact, they had Scripture in them! But it was less about what was in the books and more about my heart and where I was choosing to let my mind and emotions escape to. In 1 Corinthians 6:12, the apostle Paul writes, "It's true that our freedom allows us to do anything, but that doesn't mean that everything we do is good for us. I'm free to do as I choose, but I choose never to be enslaved to anything" (TPT). The worlds that authors create are incredible, and I believe that creativity with the written word is a gift from God. However, if I continued to choose fictional worlds filled with frilly, fancy whims as my escape when I was sad, mad, depressed, or confused, I would be disappointed again and again. Those books could not fill the void in my heart. Only Jesus could.

I know this might seem like a minor example of self-control. But sometimes weeds that appear to be small on the surface have a deep and thriving root system underground. Our hearts are similar; left unattended, things we think we can ignore become stumbling blocks. I am glad I chose to uproot my proclivity for romance books to gain a deeper and more intimate relationship with Jesus. I exchanged escapism for refuge in the Lord. And I learned to recognize when I am relying on something other than the Lord to sustain me emotionally.

Self-control is probably not the most popular fruit of the Spirit, but without practicing it, we can easily miss out on peace, patience, kindness, and faithfulness. You might find yourself in a similar situation. Maybe you are feeling a need for self-control in the area of the TV shows you watch, the video games you play, or how often you shop. It could be one of a million different things. Whatever it is, I promise that by practicing self-control in obedience to the Holy Spirit, you will receive good and perfect gifts from our heavenly Father.

PRAYER

Father, thank You for the opportunity to draw nearer to You. I come before You today with open hands and a heart ready to surrender. If there is any area in my life where I need to practice self-control, show me. Thank You that I am not on this journey alone—You will be with me every step of the way. Thank You that following Your lead will produce good fruit in my life. In Jesus' name, Amen.

FOR FURTHER STUDY

Psalm 91:9–16; 2 Peter 1:5–9; Hebrews 4:15–16

1. Did the Lord highlight an area in your life in which you need to practice self-control? As you act in obedience, don't let condemnation in. Read Romans 8:1–2 and reflect on the life-giving Spirit who has freed you.

2. Ask the Lord to show you any area of your life where you might be relying on something other than Him to sustain you. Reflect on Psalm 91:9–16. It is full of promises available to us when we make the Lord our refuge.

HOLY SPIRIT,
WHAT ARE YOU
SAYING TO
ME TODAY?

21

Taste and See

By Matthew Hernandez

Taste and see that the Lord is good.

PSALM 34:8 NIV

Something happens to me when the weather starts to turn cooler toward the end of the year. The leaves start changing, and I use words like "brisk" to describe the mornings. And it's not because I particularly like pumpkins, candles, or the cool weather that the season brings. My love for fall is centered around one thing: beef bourguignon. That's right, a meal. This is a dish my wife prepares during the fall months, and it's honestly my favorite thing in the world. Oftentimes we cook it together, dicing the onions and chopping the mushrooms while the smell of sizzling olive oil lingers throughout our kitchen. After we've chopped the beef into one-inch cubes, we throw all the ingredients in a Dutch oven, along with a bottle of red cooking wine, and let it marinate overnight. The next evening, as the dish is served over a perfectly toasted slice of sour-dough bread, I get to experience my first delicious bite of the season. In that moment, I savor the labor of our work from the evening before, and that first taste of pure goodness takes over my whole being. Yes, it really is that good! I can feel it in my soul, and it does my soul good.

Psalm 34:8 instructs us, "Taste and see that the Lord is good." Taste is about the full engagement of our senses. This Scripture invites us to experience, with everything we are, that the Lord is good. It invites us not to take someone else's word for it but to discover it for ourselves—to experience His goodness and to participate in it.

Have you ever been to a great movie, a great restaurant, or somewhere else where you had a great experience? Did you keep those experiences to yourself? No. Chances are, you told your family and friends so they could experience it as well. As followers of Jesus, the same is true for us. Because we have tasted and seen, whether through victories or trials, we can look back and see God's goodness in our life.

I love that Jesus says in John 15:4, "Remain in me, as I also remain in you. No branch can bear fruit by itself; it must remain in the vine. Neither can you bear fruit unless you remain in me" (NIV). When we remain in Jesus, whether through Scripture, prayer, or worship, we get the opportunity to "taste and see" on a regular basis. But this experience doesn't just change the life *inside* us; it also changes the culture *around* us. Jesus didn't come to earth just to teach us how to get to heaven. He came to show us a new way to live, a way in which we can show people what heaven looks like here on earth. And the more we remain—or abide—in Jesus, the more His Spirit produces fruit in us. And the more of that sweet and appealing fruit we display to the people around us, the more opportunities they have to "taste and see" just how good the Lord who lives within you and me is.

Think about your coworkers, classmates, friends, and neighbors. Is there anyone whose life would change if they experienced the love of Jesus? What would happen if we lived our lives in such a way that pointed others to experience God's grace, love, and mercy for themselves? Then they, too, could experience with their whole being just how good the God of the universe is.

Friends, may you remain in the love of God. May you taste and see His goodness with your heart and soul, and may this experience give you the courage to live a life that points others to experience Him as well!

PRAYER

God, Your Word says in Psalm 119:68, "You are good, and what You do is good." Thank You for being such a wonderful Father who cares for His children in both big and small ways. Help us to turn hearts toward You as we experience Your perfect love. May we honor You as we share the joy of knowing You with the people You bring into our lives. In Jesus' name, Amen.

FOR FURTHER STUDY

John 15:1–17; Psalm 31:19–20

FOR FURTHER REFLECTION

1. When was the last time you experienced the goodness of God? How did this experience change you?

2. Which individuals in your life right now do you want to "taste and see that the Lord is good"? Begin praying for God to show you ways that you can be a light in those people's lives and show them glimpses of heaven.

HOLY SPIRIT, WHAT ARE YOU SAYING TO ME TODAY?

Memory
Verses

By their fruit you will recognize them. Do people pick grapes from thornbushes, or figs from thistles? Likewise, every good tree bears good fruit, but a bad tree bears bad fruit. A good tree cannot bear bad fruit, and a bad tree cannot bear good fruit.

....

**MATTHEW 7:16-18
NIV**

But the Holy Spirit produces this kind of fruit in our lives: love, joy, peace, patience, kindness, goodness, faithfulness, gentleness, and self-control. There is no law against these things! Those who belong to Christ Jesus have nailed the passions and desires of their sinful nature to his cross and crucified them there. Since we are living by the Spirit, let us follow the Spirit's leading in every part of our lives.

....

**GALATIANS 5:22-25
NLT**

Abide in Me, and I in you. As the branch cannot bear fruit of itself, unless it abides in the vine, neither can you, unless you abide in Me. I am the vine, you are the branches. He who abides in Me, and I in him, bears much fruit; for without Me you can do nothing.

....

**JOHN 15:4-5
NKJV**

3

2

1